LOW-FAT
ONE-DISH MEALS
from around the World

BY

JANE MARSH DIECKMANN

 The Crossing Press
Freedom, California 95019

Library of Congress Cataloging-in-Publication Data

Dieckmann, Jane Marsh.
    Low-fat, one-dish meals from around the world / Jane Marsh Dieckmann
        p. cm.
    Includes index.
    ISBN 0-89594-608-4 — ISBN 0-89594-607-6 (pbk.)
    1. Cookery, International   2. Casserole cookery.   3. Low-fat diet—Recipes.
    I. Title.
TX725.A1D477   1993
641.59—dc20
                                                 92-43485
                                             CIP

This book is dedicated to you who are interested in good, healthful food from different traditions, and especially to Inge and Walter, who represent the international at its very best.

Contents

Introduction

When I was growing up (back in the Middle Ages, my daughters are wont to say), the evening meal consisted of meat, a starch (almost always potatoes or white rice), a vegetable, and a salad. We rarely ate fish, pasta was almost completely unknown, and anything faintly hinting of ethnic or foreign cuisine simply did not exist at our table. We did live in the country and had a vegetable garden, so, at least during the summer months, freshly picked vegetables were part of the meal. Unfortunately many of the ones we ate were very well cooked; my father was a Southerner and, in his tradition, al dente, crisp, or chewy was not acceptable. We ate a lot meat, much of it roasted, and a lot of gravy and butter.

Times have changed indeed. Until only recently six to eight ounces of beef was considered the normal individual portion. Today, that amount can serve three or four and often more—fortunately for our health and welfare, not to mention the health and welfare of the planet—even in the fanciest and most expensive dishes. To compensate, the portion size and general use of vegetables and grains have increased enormously. Bulgur, for example, of which I knew nothing until I was in my late twenties, is now an important staple in my pantry and part of my diet.

Eating Well in Today's World

The current trends in food preparation and consumption point to several interesting phenomena. More and more people are eating at home—for convenience, because of time constraints and scheduling, for reasons of economy, and, especially important, because of nutrition and health considerations. A good number of us simply enjoy eating at home. We like the idea of knowing what we will be eating and how it is prepared; we like knowing when we'll be able to start and finish the meal; and we like the challenge of putting together something healthful that our family will find tasty and appealing. Eating at home can be fun and creative, if we understand that cooking a good dinner doesn't have to mean running a race or putting on a juggling act or necessarily creating an aesthetically exceptional work of art.

As to nutrition and health, cooks today must face several serious concerns. An increasingly important one is for clean and safe food. Although we cannot always have absolute control over what we eat, purchasing or growing food and preparing it ourselves lower the potential risks from contamination and additives. Closely connected is the concern for freshness. We should all aim to use fresh fruits, vegetables, and seafood rather than canned or frozen. And for adding flavor to health and nutrition issues, how about minced or crushed fresh garlic or fresh ginger (rather than the dried or ground varieties), freshly squeezed lemon juice, and freshly ground pepper? The general growing interest in fresh ingredients is seen in the produce sections of our supermarkets, with widely diverse offerings of vegetables and fruits, greens, and herbs from every corner of the earth.

Attentive homemakers are also concerned with preparing healthy meals that contain less fat, salt, and other additives of dubious nutritional value. At the same time inventive cooks are exploring ethnic cuisines, taking advantage of the many dishes coming from diverse cultures while using this inspiring variety of ingredients now available.

In keeping with these trends, here is a collection of recipes for low-fat, healthful main dishes featuring fresh ingredients, nutrition-rich legumes and grains, and a broad spectrum of international flavors.

The recipes contain the principal elements of a meal, usually cooked in one pot—in the oven or on the top of the stove. In many cases, the meal can be served right out of the cooking receptacle. The addition of a salad or simple side dish, hearty bread, and a beverage completes the meal. The emphasis here is on simplicity of preparation, the combination of fresh and wholesome ingredients, and the borrowing of old and new ideas from different cooking traditions worldwide. Here you can find many easy solutions for eating wisely and for combining different flavors and textures.

What Is Low-fat Anyway?

High cholesterol, high blood pressure, obesity, heart disease, and many types of cancer are related to the types of food we eat. Even healthy people who successfully control their weight want a wholesome diet that will keep them fit. We should all eat a variety of foods, keep a healthy weight, and choose a diet that is low in fat—especially low in saturated fat and cholesterol. We should eat plenty of vegetables, grain products, and fruits. We should use only moderate amounts of salt, sodium products, and sugar. The dietary guidelines for lower cancer risk, for example, suggest only moderate consumption of salt-cured, salt-pickled, and smoked foods; substitution of whole wheat flour for all-purpose flour in recipes for baked products; use of brown rice instead of white rice; and consumption of more vitamin- and beta-carotine-rich vegetables, such as broccoli, chard, peppers, spinach, carrots, sweet potatoes, and winter squash.

Here are the basics to understanding the issues of cholesterol and "good" fats versus "bad" fats—issues that bewilder even the most well-informed people. Not all fats clog arteries and not all fats contain cholesterol, a substance that accumulates in deposits in the arteries, eventually restricting blood flow to the heart. Cholesterol is found in meat (especially red meat), egg yolks, and such dairy products as butter, cream, cheese, and whole milk. Saturated fats—so called because they are "saturated" with hydrogen—increase the risk of heart disease; eating them raises blood levels of cholesterol. Many vegetable products are labeled as containing no cholesterol, even though vegetables do not contain cholesterol anyway. However, a few—for example, tropical oils, often used in commercial baked products and some coffee creamers—are high in saturated fats. Even though they contain no cholesterol, they are capable of raising blood cholesterol levels because they contain saturated fats.

Hence we should avoid tropical oils, such as coconut and palm oil, and cut down drastically on butter, cheese (especially cheese with a high fat content), whole eggs, and red meat. In a healthy diet these foods would be replaced by more grains, fruits, vegetables, fish, and poultry and such dairy products as skim milk, low- or reduced-fat cheeses, and low-fat or nonfat yogurt. Keep in mind that grains, legumes, fresh vegetables, and fruits contain no cholesterol at all, and most contain no fat at all, the notable exceptions being peanuts and avocados.

Although the jury is still out on many questions concerning fats and the ways our bodies use them, medical researchers agree that monounsaturated oils—olive oil, peanut oil, and canola oil—represent a better health bet than polyunsaturated oils—corn oil, soybean oil, safflower oil, and other vegetable oils. Of the monounsaturated oils, canola oil has the lowest amount of saturated fat. The best health bet is using less fat altogether, regardless of whether it is saturated, polyunsaturated, or monounsaturated.

Here are some ways to think lean when you cook. (Remember, many recipes you currently use can be adapted to lean preparation.)

- Steam, boil, poach, bake, microwave, or broil foods instead of sautéing or frying them. If you do sauté and the recipe calls for oil, do not grease the pan at all; if the recipe specifies no oil, grease a nonstick pan very lightly with oil or try a vegetable spray.

- Avoid rich sauces that use a lot of fat.

- Make your own salad dressings, using less oil than called for, or no oil, replacing it with more vinegar (try a milder flavor such as balsamic vinegar) or broth (chicken or vegetable) or—what I like best of all—plain low-fat yogurt.

- Use less meat overall, use leaner cuts, and trim off all visible fat. With chicken, remove the skin, especially if you are cooking it in liquid.

Seasoning

Most people should minimize the amount of salt in their diet. The recipes in this book emphasize flavoring with vegetables, fruits, herbs, and spices instead of salt. To my taste, a few drops of freshly squeezed lemon juice on lightly cooked fresh green beans tastes better than butter and salt. Here are some ways to cut down on your salt intake.

- Make your own meat, chicken, and vegetable stocks (see pages 146 and 147 for recipes and hints). If you must use commercial stocks, purchase the low-sodium varieties that contain the least number of additives.

- Avoid salted and smoked meat products; if you use ham in a recipe, don't add any salt.

- Use the low-sodium version of condiments and flavorings, such as low-sodium soy sauce, hot sauce, and salad dressing.

Basic Ingredients

Meat
The general rule for beef, pork, and lamb is to use less of it. Purchase the leaner cuts (they are often less expensive anyway) and trim off any visible fat. The lean cuts of beef (from leanest to fattest) are top round, eye of round, round tip, sirloin, top loin, and tenderloin. Lean veal, though expensive, is very lean indeed, with the leg and sirloin the leanest cuts.

Lamb is a fatty meat but, because it is less marbled than beef, it is easier to trim off much of the fat. Do serve smaller portions, though. The leg of lamb and loin chops are the leanest cuts. Lamb shanks, when trimmed of fat, make an excellent stew, high in flavor and protein.

The lean cuts of pork (from leanest to fattest) are tenderloin, boneless sirloin chop, boneless loin roast and chops, boneless top loin, loin, and rib. Avoid bacon, ham, sausages, and hotdogs, unless you can find a truly low-fat variety. They all come in turkey versions and have a good flavor, especially when cooked with other foods in casseroles and stews, but they still contain considerable fat and many possibly harmful additives. My advice is to use these meats rather than the traditional pork versions, but in small quantities.

Ground beef comes in various categories of lean; 95 percent lean contains three times less fat per gram after cooking than does 80 percent lean. Purchase the leanest you can find, or buy a lean cut and grind it yourself. Avoid ground pork and lamb unless you can have it ground for you personally from very lean cuts. Many cooks use ground turkey or—for a non-fat, high-protein alternative—ground cooked soybeans.

Poultry
White meat chicken and turkey are relatively low in fat, especially if you don't eat the skin. Dark meat is higher in fat, although turkey legs and wings are leaner than chicken drumsticks and wings. The consensus among researchers is that removing the skin before cooking poultry will dry out the meat considerably, whereas leaving the skin on does not add noticeable fat to the dish, provided you remove the skin before eating.

Seafood

A considerable attention getter these days is omega-3 oil, found in finfish, which seems to help prevent blood clots. As a general rule, eat a variety of seafood and in moderation. Fish highest in omega-3 oils are salmon, mackerel, herring, and sardines; trout contains a lesser amount.

Shellfish that are stationary on the ocean floor—including clams, mussels, oysters, and scallops—contain only a small amount of cholesterol. Crustaceans that are mobile—crabs, crayfish, shrimp, and lobsters—contain some cholesterol but are quite low in saturated fat, shrimp containing the most. Moderate consumption is the key, not to mention what you put on the seafood; so remember to hold the butter and forget the deep frying.

Remember too that it is economical and time saving to purchase and cook more meat, poultry, and seafood than you will need for one meal. The possibilities for using leftovers are numerous and make a fine challenge to the creative cook.

Vegetables

All dietary guidelines recommend eating fresh vegetables. From childhood we learned that Popeye the Sailor got his strength from eating spinach, and that eating carrots would help us see in the dark. No matter the stories and legends, vegetables are good for you and, for the most part, low in calories. Certainly for a lean meal, they are essential.

Recent research points to the benefits of the dark green and orange vegetables and to the beta-carotene they contain, which is believed to protect against cancer. Beta-carotene is one of a large group of substances called carotenoids, which are generally found in the same vegetables and fruits, and which may also have anticancer properties. Why not include in your diet such orange and yellow vegetables and fruits as carrots, sweet potatoes, winter squash, pumpkin, mangoes, cantaloupe, and apricots, and such green vegetables as kale, spinach, broccoli, Swiss chard, and green bell peppers?

Fresh summer vegetables should be eaten fresh; not only do they taste better, their nutritional value is higher. Frozen vegetables are a great boon to the home cook, however, and come in a wide variety, from artichokes to turnip greens. Many of the more frequently consumed vegetables come frozen in bags of a pound or more. If you have freezer space, these are a good buy and are useful because you can take out the amount you need, close the bag, and refreeze the remainder for use at another time.

The so-called winter vegetables—such as potatoes, sweet potatoes, onions, garlic, winter squash, carrots, beets, turnips, and parsnips—can be stored in a cool place and used when needed. Some store well for six months or more.

If you must purchase canned vegetables, look for the reduced-salt or salt-free versions. When fresh tomatoes are not in season, canned tomatoes are often better than the "plastic" tomatoes found in supermarkets. Tomatoes come canned in sauce, pureed, whole and crushed, regular, and Italian plum. I find whole tomatoes the easiest to deal with; they are often the most economical too.

Potatoes are an important part of the lean diet; they contain very little fat and are a good source of vitamin C, the B vitamins, and potassium. Yet the potato is thought by many to be fattening because it is high in carbohydrates. Are these the people who can contemplate a baked potato only when it is topped with sour cream or loads of butter? Not the potato's fault, is it? Try a baked potato with Yogurt Herb Topping (page 150).

Legumes

A staple food in most cuisines all over the world, legumes are economical, easily prepared, and brimming with nutrition in the form of protein, complex carbohydrates, vitamins, and minerals. There are many kinds of legumes, including red, white, black, pink, and mottled beans, not to mention lentils, chick-peas (garbanzos), yellow and green split peas, and soybeans, which contain more protein than any of the others.

The best way to serve legumes is to combine them with grains, providing "complete" proteins with no cholesterol and very little fat. Many legumes are available canned, but they have added salt and a mushy consistency. If you must use canned (sometimes the quick, easy solution simply works better), be sure to rinse and drain them well. It is easy to prepare your own, however, although it does take some time. See page 145 for cooking methods and yields.

Grains and Pasta

International traditions have added immeasurably to our knowledge and use of grains in cooking. In addition to rice, we have bulgur, barley, millet, couscous, and quinoa, not to mention grain by-products such as grain flours, rolled grains, corn-meal, and wheat germ—truly an endless bounty.

Rice

One could write an entire book on cooking with all the different kinds of rice available today and its use in every possible cooking tradition. There are more than 40,000 varieties of rice in the world, the most used being long- and short-grain brown and white rice, aromatic rices, and rice blends. Long-grain rice, the type traditionally preferred in the United States, cooks dry and fluffy, with separate grains. Short-grain rice, the rice of choice in parts of Asia and the Mediterranean, is moist, clingy, and soft after cooking. Arborio, used to make the Italian dish risotto, is a short-grain rice.

Among the aromatic rices, the best known is the Indian rice called basmati, grown for centuries in Pakistan and northern India. It has a distinctive and appealing aroma and subtle flavor, making it a favorite for Middle Eastern and exotic Indian dishes. The Americanized version of basmati is called texmati, with a nutty flavor and an aroma similar to freshly popped corn. Wehani, by contrast, has the scent of hot buttered peanuts, and is earthy in flavor and honey red in color; it is often sold in rice blends. Wild pecan is a long-grain rice that contains no nuts despite its name, which comes from the rice's nutty flavor and aroma.

Long-grain and short-grain rice and basmati and texmati rice are sold in brown and white versions. Brown rice retains its outer bran and its germ; because of this it has more vitamins and minerals than plain milled rice and, because of its fatty germ, derives 4 percent of its calories from fat. That's not much fat, however, and remember, there is no cholesterol in any rice.

White rice has been milled to remove the bran and germ, and contains only a trace of fat. If enriched, it can have more nutrients than the natural brown product. All rice is good source of B vitamins. The most nutritious way to serve rice is with legumes, since the combination produces complete protein. Rice is also more nutritious when served with meat or a food rich in vitamin C (tomatoes and peppers, for example), because these foods increase the availability of the iron in the rice.

Wild rice is not a true member of the rice family but the seed of a native American grass. It is expensive to gather and mill, so it is often mixed with other rices to make it more economical. It does have a wonderful and unusual flavor.

Barley

This grain is the mainstay of many baked dishes and soups. A small grain, probably the most ancient of cultivated cereals, barley is grown over a wider climatic range than any other grain. Removing the husk results in pearl barley, which cooks more quickly but is lower in nutrients and fiber than whole barley. Whole barley can be presoaked for several hours before cooking, thus cutting down on preparation time.

Bulgur

The preferred grain of central Europe and the Middle East, bulgur is widely used in many dishes and is, of course, the principal ingredient of tabouli. Bulgur is made by first boiling, then drying and grinding whole wheat. It is available fine or coarse ground. Cooking time is about 20 minutes and when you make tabouli, you don't cook the bulgur at all!

Other Grains

Millet has been cultivated since prehistoric times in Asia, northern Africa, and southern Europe. Today it is cultivated in Asia and parts of Europe. The most noticeable ingredient in mixed bird seed, millet is also a delicious and quick-cooking grain, with a little crunch.

Quinoa, also an ancient grain, comes from Peru, and has a nutty, almost sweet flavor. It looks similar to millet; simmer it for about 30 minutes.

Couscous is small, golden grains of semolina and is normally cooked by steaming (see page 93 for directions). It is often served with spicy stew.

Orzo, a Greek type of durum wheat pasta, is shaped like rice. It cooks easily and quickly. Follow the indications for cooking pasta (page 46).

Consult page 145 in the Appendix for a timetable and indications for cooking whole grains.

Pasta

Pasta comes in many—and often beautiful—shapes and sizes. It also comes in many flavors and colors, ranging from the greens of the spinach and pesto pastas to the pale orange red of the tomato pasta to the charcoal of the squid pasta. Shapes include spirals, elbows, tubes, little wheels, bow ties, and shells, long and short, thin and broad. The healthiest way to eat pasta is with fresh beans and peas and the legumes. Most commonly, it is eaten with meat and cheese. See page 46 for cooking indications.

Basically pasta consists of water plus flour and/or semolina (the coarsely milled inner part of the wheat kernel, called the endosperm—the more semolina the pasta contains, the more protein it has). In addition to the most common forms, pasta comes made of whole wheat flour and in a high-protein form fortified with soy flour. Egg noodles, as their name indicates, are made with flour and water plus eggs. (Those with cholesterol problems should avoid egg noodles.) In Asian cuisines are found rice noodles, made with rice flour, and cellophane noodles, made with flour ground from sprouted mung beans.

Dairy Products

Cheese, that delicious and popular ingredient, can make the low-fat part rather difficult. The following will help you cook lean with cheese: Cheeses very high in fat (70 percent or more of the calories being derived from fat) are American, blue, Camembert, Cheddar, colby, cream cheese, feta, Muenster, Neufchâtel, and Parmesan. Cheeses moderately high in fat (50 to 70 percent of calories) include provolone, ricotta (both whole milk and part-skim, the latter having a lower percentage of fat), Romano, and mozzarella. Cheeses with a low fat content (20 to 35 percent of calories) are cottage cheese (regular and low-fat), pot cheese, and farmer cheese. (Cottage cheese is also available in a nonfat version.)

Although there are some fairly good low-fat versions of normally high-fat cheeses, there are also some fairly awful ones. Unfortunately, removing the fat from the cheese often produces something akin to rubber. My advice is to try out what you can find in your market and see how you like it. There is excellent part-skim mozzarella cheese, for example, as well as reduced-fat and low-fat ricotta (reduced-fat has half the fat of low-fat), cottage cheese, and yogurt. There are also nonfat varieties of yogurt (though I find nonfat plain yogurt to have less "yogurt" flavor than the low-fat variety). Farmer cheese and pot cheese are very low in fat. Use these products whenever possible. Beware, though, of the label "lite"; it usually means a little less fat than the normal product, a different flavor and consistency, and a lot of additives.

Sap Sago, an aged Swiss skim-milk cheese, is now available in the United States. A cheese for grating, it comes in a small cone-shaped, silver-papered package and has a lovely pale green color and a robust flavor. It is expensive, but because of its intense flavor, a little goes a long way. It makes a good topping for pasta or cooked vegetables. Look also for reduced-fat Jarlsberg, Swiss, Cheddar, and Monterey jack cheeses.

For lean cooking, use smaller quantities of whatever cheese you select. When making sauces and toppings, use grated rather than sliced cheese. This results in using less (hence less fat) overall but with a barely noticeable difference in flavor.

As for milk, whenever possible use skim milk or canned evaporated skimmed milk. Nonfat dry milk can often be stirred into dishes to boost protein and calcium without adding any fat. Avoid cream of all kinds, as well as whole milk, even 2 percent milk, which seems low in fat but really isn't.

Seasonings

The flavor of many dishes is enhanced by the addition of herbs and spices; indeed, seasonings sometimes determine a characteristic flavor or ethnic history of a dish. Curry is associated with Indian and Southeast Asian cooking, chiles with Mexican food, oregano and basil with dishes from the Mediterranean. When using herbs and spices, remember to season judiciously. You can never take out what has been added, but you can always add more. Sometimes combining too many herbs defeats the purpose of the seasoning, and no distinctive flavor will prevail. Remember too that seasoning with herbs and spices often compensates for using less salt, as we know, a healthy aim.

Use fresh herbs whenever possible, remembering that you need a greater quantity of fresh than dried herbs (about three times more) because the flavor is not so concentrated. Before adding fresh herbs, either mince them finely or rub the herbs between your fingers to release the flavors. Recipes for various herb and spice combinations are given in the Appendix.

Equipment

Here are some suggestions for equipment that you might find useful for the recipes given here and that I have found particularly helpful when preparing them.

Baking Dishes, Pots, Pans, and Bowls

For meals prepared in the oven, you will need several different kinds of baking dishes. Heavy glass dishes, round, square, or rectangular, are ideal for pies, lasagne, and open casseroles. A good pottery casserole dish with a cover is a must. The most useful baking utensil of all, I find, is a heavy Dutch oven—either black cast iron or another metal, often with a brightly colored enamel covering. The advantage is that it goes from stove top to oven, so you can sauté some ingredients, then add the others, and bake everything together, all in the same pot.

For stove-top cooking, you will need nonaluminum saucepans in several sizes. A Dutch oven is wonderful for stews, chili, and many grain dishes. It should be heavy—in fact, the heavier the pot, the less likely that grains and other ingredients will burn on the bottom.

For skillet dishes, a skillet with a tight-fitting lid is needed, preferably in small and large sizes. For stir-frying, a wok is ideal, especially for lean cooking, because very little fat is necessary in the hot central area. In our kitchen we have found a large pan with cover called a sauté or Peking pan very useful—

it's a cross between a wok and a skillet, being somewhat bowl-shaped. Ours is 12 inches in diameter and 3 inches high, and it accommodates just about any food. Look for utensils with nonstick finishes and you'll need only a minimum of fat.

For soups, a good heavy stockpot, 6 quarts or larger in size, is recommended. Although a Dutch oven or stew pot will also work for soups, a larger pot is useful if you prepare large quantities of stock at a time.

For salads, low and broad is an easier shape to work with than tall and deep. You can mix everything much more quickly. Do try to find a pretty salad serving bowl.

Useful Kitchen Tools and Appliances

A good pressure cooker is very useful, especially for cooking legumes (see the Appendix). Every kitchen should have a mixer, blender, and food processor to save time and energy, especially when you are chopping a lot of vegetables or pureeing liquids. A minichopper comes in handy for small jobs—chopping parsley, green onions, and fresh herbs. (Of course you can always put the parsley or herbs in a coffee cup and mince them with kitchen scissors.)

A salad spinner is a great help if you prepare a lot of salads. After having used a large one (10 inches in diameter) for years—it's wonderful for large meals and parties—I invested in an 8-inch model, which I use all the time for the daily salad.

A steamer insert is indispensable when preparing vegetables. (If you blanch vegetables for freezing, you probably already have a blancher with a steam insert, which will come in handy). Several cutting boards are recommended; keep a plastic one for cutting chicken and meats, so that it can be well cleaned). Kitchen scissors and good sharp knives are essential. Carbon steel, although it discolors and is hard to find, still makes the best knives. You may

want to have several long- and short-handled wooden spoons and those marvelous bowl-shaped rubber scrapers called spoonolas (they come in two sizes). I find Pyrex measuring cups, in 4-cup, 2-cup, and 1-cup sizes, to be useful. They work both on the stove top and in the microwave and serve well to measure and mix in the same container, especially in the 4-cup size. A food scale is also very helpful.

A Final Bit of Philosophy

This book presents appealing, comfortable food from various cooking traditions, prepared in an easy-going and uncomplicated way that reflects our need for a less frantic pace in the kitchen—all with the understanding that both our time and the quality of our lives are important.

The approach of the book is experimental and adventuresome. It encourages you to try various interesting and often unusual and unfamiliar combinations, adapting the best and most fruitful ideas to your own individual cooking and using what works well for you.

Cooking should be fun and relaxed; a meal should be enjoyed by everyone—including the cook—and consumed in a leisurely fashion. With good planning and ideas like those in this book, you should have time to sit down and relax before dinner, enjoy a conversation with the family, read the paper, and be ready to appreciate the good meal coming up.

Although I have made much of cooking good, wholesome, everyday meals for the whole family to enjoy, most dishes here can be served at a dinner party with pride. These meals are healthful and nutritious, delicious, and—above all—interesting. So in whatever language you want to say it and in whatever tradition you want to cook it, enjoy what follows and know that you are eating to your good health.

Casseroles & Other Oven-Cooked Dishes

Except in the hottest months of the year, using the oven to prepare main dishes is a simple and economical way to cook dinner. Over the years I have relied more and more on the oven stew—in which meat, poultry, or fish cooks gently along with accompanying vegetables—or the casserole, in which various elements of a meal are combined and baked. In either case, the cook can relax while the meal almost magically prepares itself, all the while putting out savory smells from the kitchen.

The casserole has gained popularity as a one-dish meal, especially since the 1950s when new forms of lightweight earthenware and glassware appeared on the market. The word *casserole* is a French term for a cooking utensil made of metal or other ovenproof material, fitted with a lid and designed for long, slow cooking in the oven. Today the name applies to the meal cooked therein—a baked dish, combining several ingredients, frequently a complete meal.

Oven cooking has many advantages: Meals can be prepared in advance, leaving some free time at the dinner hour; they are economical, often combining low-cost and/or leftover foods in unusual and uncomplicated ways; and they can be served from the dish in which they are cooked (and also later stored if left over). And on a cold winter evening, what could be a more pleasant and better way to warm your kitchen?

Ziti Casserole

A variation on lasagne, this has been a favorite dish in my household for years. Serve it with a salad of mixed, slightly bitter greens, crusty Italian bread, and Italian red wine—chianti or bardolino.

1 pound ziti or penne
2 cups reduced-fat ricotta cheese
4 ounces part-skim mozzarella cheese, diced
1/4 cup freshly grated Romano cheese
1 egg, beaten
10 ounces fresh spinach, washed, stems removed, leaves chopped
1/3 cup chopped flat-leaf (Italian) parsley
1/2 teaspoon salt
1/4 teaspoon freshly ground black pepper
6 cups Spaghetti Sauce (page 148)

Cook the pasta according to directions on page 46; drain.

Meanwhile, in a large bowl combine the cheeses, egg, spinach, parsley, salt, and ground pepper. Pour a little of the Spaghetti Sauce in the bottom of a rectangular baking dish or 3-quart casserole; then layer the drained pasta, spinach filling, and the remaining Spaghetti Sauce. Bake at 350 degrees F until the sauce is bubbly (about 40 minutes). Serve at once.

Serves 8.

New England Oven Pot Roast

This dish has been part of American cooking for years. It can be prepared in many ways, reflecting other culinary traditions. This pot roast is a basic version. The cooking pot should be flameproof, deep, and heavy, with a tight cover. A heavy Dutch oven is ideal. Serve this meal with crusty whole-grain bread or, if you want to follow New England tradition, Skinny Corn Bread (page 152), a robust red wine or beer, and, if you like, a salad of sliced tomatoes and greens with a tangy vinaigrette dressing.

1 tablespoon canola oil
1 tablespoon all-purpose flour
1 teaspoon salt
1/4 teaspoon freshly ground white or black
   pepper
1/4 teaspoon sugar (to help brown the meat)
1 piece beef (about 3 pounds), preferably top
   round, all visible fat removed
2 cloves garlic, sliced
3 large onions, sliced
1 1/2 cups water
1 bay leaf
3 large carrots, cut into thirds lengthwise, then
   quartered
4 potatoes, cut into slices or chunks
1 teaspoon dried rosemary
1 teaspoon dried thyme
2 tablespoons chopped parsley

In a heavy flameproof pot over medium-high heat, warm the oil. Combine the flour, salt, ground pepper, and sugar and sprinkle it over the meat, rubbing it in. Brown the meat in the oil, turning it often, until it turns a deep brown color (about 20 minutes).

Reduce the heat to medium-low and add the garlic and onions. Cook until they have browned slightly. Stir in the water and bay leaf, scraping to deglaze the pot, then cover and place the pot in a 300 degree F oven. Cook for about 2 hours.

Add the carrots, potatoes, rosemary, and thyme and cook until the beef is tender and the vegetables are done (about 2 hours).

Remove the pot from the oven. Remove and discard the bay leaf. Cut the meat into thin slices and arrange on a serving platter with the vegetables. Sprinkle the parsley over all and serve hot.

Serves 6 to 8.

Note: If you have some of this left over, slice the meat thinly and cut the vegetables into small pieces. Combine everything with Lentils, Monastery Style (page 92) for a hearty mixed vegetable stew or, if you prefer something hotter and spicier, with Garden Vegetable Curry (page 68).

Variations

Oven Pot Roast, Mexican Style. Omit the water; substitute 2 cups canned tomatoes with juice. With the potatoes add 1 sliced green bell pepper, 1 cup fresh corn kernels cut from the cob, 3 finely chopped tomatillos, and 2 1/2 tablespoons chopped green chiles. Instead of the dried herbs, add 1 teaspoon chili powder and 1/2 teaspoon ground cumin. Substitute 1 tablespoon minced cilantro for the parsley.

Oven Pot Roast, German Style. Substitute 2 cups beer for the water. With the vegetables add 1 teaspoon grated lemon zest and 1 pound fresh mushrooms, sliced. If desired, thicken the sauce with 1 tablespoon all-purpose flour mixed with 2 tablespoons water.

Beef Potato Moussaka

This popular Greek (or, according to some, Turkish) dish has traditionally used whatever is fresh in the garden (or, perhaps, left over in the refrigerator). This simplified version uses beef and zucchini. Serve it with a Greek salad with ripe olives and a little crumbled feta cheese, topped with Creamy Vinaigrette (page 149).

4 medium potatoes, halved
3/4 pound lean ground beef
1 medium onion, chopped
1 large clove garlic, minced
2 cups Tomato Sauce (page 147) or diced canned
    tomatoes
1/2 teaspoon dried oregano
1/4 teaspoon ground cinnamon
1/4 teaspoon salt
1/4 freshly ground white pepper
4 cups thinly sliced zucchini
1/4 cup skim milk
1 cup plain nonfat yogurt
2 eggs *or* 1/2 cup egg substitute
1/2 cup shredded part-skim mozzarella cheese

In a large saucepan over high heat, boil the potatoes in water to cover for about 5 minutes. Drain and set aside.

In the same pan over medium heat, lightly brown the beef, onion, and garlic. Drain off any fat. Add the Tomato Sauce, oregano, cinnamon, salt, and ground pepper; cover and let simmer for about 20 minutes.

Slice the reserved potatoes about 1/4 inch thick and arrange half of them in a rectangular baking dish. Cover with the zucchini slices and pour the tomato-meat mixture over all. Top with the remaining potato slices.

Measure the milk and yogurt into a 2-cup measure and beat in the eggs. Pour over the potato slices,

then sprinkle with the cheese. Bake at 350 degrees F for about 30 minutes. Let stand for 15 minutes before serving.

Serves 6 to 8.

Variations

Lamb Eggplant Moussaka. Substitute 1/2 pound lean ground lamb (either cooked or uncooked) for the beef. Substitute 1 large eggplant, peeled and sliced, for the zucchini. Pat the eggplant slices dry on paper towels and cut them into small pieces, if desired. Cook the eggplant with the potatoes. Save the outside slices to arrange on the top layer.

Vegetarian Moussaka. Instead of meat, substitute navy beans (see the Appendix for cooking directions: Use 6 cups water, 2/3 cup dried navy beans, 1 bay leaf, 4 fresh sage leaves, and 3 cloves garlic; drain, remove the bay leaf, and add the beans to the sauce). Add 1/4 cup red wine to the sauce and use both eggplant and zucchini in layers as the vegetables.

Beef and Bulgur, Mediterranean Style

Here is a tasty, herb-flavored combination, using a chewy grain for its base. Serve it with a mixed green salad.

1/2 pound lean ground beef
1 large onion, chopped
1 large clove garlic, minced
1 1/2 cups bulgur
3 cups boiling water
3 tablespoons chopped parsley, or more to taste
1 teaspoon Italian Herb Blend (page 150)
1/2 teaspoon celery seed
1/2 teaspoon salt
1/4 teaspoon freshly ground mixed pepper
2 large tomatoes, diced
2 cups julienned young fresh green beans *or*
    1 package (10 ounces) frozen French green
    beans, defrosted
1/4 cup grated Romano or Sap Sago cheese, or
    more to taste

In a heavy flameproof pot, sauté the beef, onion, and garlic, breaking up the meat and cooking until it is firm. Drain off any excess fat. Stir in the bulgur, boiling water, parsley, herb blend, celery seed, salt, ground pepper, tomatoes, and green beans. Cover and bake at 350 degrees F for about 30 minutes.

Uncover, sprinkle the cheese over the top, and continue baking for another 15 minutes. Garnish with additional chopped parsley and cheese, if desired, and serve hot.

Serves 4.

Tamale Pie

The term *tamale* describes many different dishes based on a cornmeal dough placed inside corn husks and then steamed. Mexican in origin, tamales were enjoyed by the Aztecs. The tamale pie is a longtime southwestern favorite. Serve it with lightly cooked fresh green beans with a squeeze of lime and freshly ground white pepper.

3 cups skim milk
2 cups cornmeal
1 pound lean ground beef
1 large onion, chopped
1 clove garlic, minced
1 can (28 ounces) whole tomatoes, chopped, with
    liquid
2 cups cooked corn kernels *or* 1 can (16 ounces)
    whole kernel corn, drained
1 tablespoon chili powder
1/2 teaspoon ground cumin
1/2 teaspoon dried oregano
1 cup pitted ripe olives, drained
1 cup shredded reduced-fat Cheddar or Monterey
    jack cheese

In a large saucepan with a lid, mix the milk with the cornmeal and cook over medium heat until thickened. Line the bottom and sides of a lightly oiled 3-quart casserole or 13- by 9-inch baking dish with the cornmeal mush. Set aside.

Wash out and dry the cooking pan. Brown together the ground beef, onion, and garlic; drain off any excess fat. Stir in the tomatoes, corn, chili powder, cumin, and oregano. Cover and simmer for 15 minutes. Remove from heat and stir in the olives.

Spoon the tomato mixture on top of the cornmeal and top with the shredded cheese. Bake, uncovered, at 350 degrees F until the pie is bubbling and the cheese is browned (40 to 45 minutes). Serve hot.

Serves 8.

Lasagne, Easy and Modern

Lasagne has been a tradition in Italian cooking for many years, and a great variety (and rivalry) exists between northern and southern styles. For those who live in the United States, lasagne has become the mainstay of the potluck supper, the Boy Scout banquet, or any gathering where hungry people gather to eat a hearty meal. The easy and modern part of this lasagne is that you do not cook the pasta in advance, thus saving time and energy. Although lasagne isn't exactly the leanest of foods, you can help make it so by using the leanest ground beef, mozzarella, and cottage cheese you can find. For a truly low-fat version, try the Eggplant Lasagne (page 40). Serve lasagne with a mixed green salad, crusty Italian bread, and hearty Italian red wine.

2 ounces mild Italian turkey sausage
12 ounces lean ground beef
6 cups Marinara Sauce (page 147)
2 cups nonfat cottage cheese
1 egg
2 cups hot water
12 ounces uncooked wide lasagne noodles,
  spinach or whole wheat
1 cup shredded part-skim mozzarella cheese
1/4 cup grated Romano or Asiago cheese

Remove the sausage from its casing and chop the meat into small pieces. In a large skillet over medium heat, brown it with the ground beef, breaking up lumps with a fork. Remove the meat and drain it on paper towels; then wipe out the pan well.

Pour in the sauce and mix in the meat. Bring to a simmer and cook, partially covered, for about 2 hours. You can make this sauce in advance.

Measure the cottage cheese into a 4-cup measure and beat the egg into it.

Spread a little meat sauce in the bottom of a 13-by 9-inch baking dish. Mix in 1 cup of the hot water. Add a layer of noodles, then spoon some cottage cheese-egg mixture down the center of each noodle. Cover with sauce, then sprinkle with the mozzarella. Repeat these layers twice. Sprinkle with the grated Romano. Pour the remaining 1 cup hot water evenly over all. Cover tightly with aluminum foil and bake in a 400 degree F oven for 30 minutes.

Remove the foil. The pasta will be almost tender and a lot of liquid will remain in the pan. Continue to bake, uncovered, until the cheese topping is browned and most of the liquid is absorbed (10 to 20 minutes). Allow the lasagne to stand for 15 minutes before serving.

Serves 8.

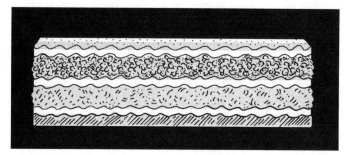

Lasagne in the Microwave

This version of lasagne is leaner and much quicker than the previous one, since the sauce needs no lengthy cooking time and the cook can benefit from the speed of the microwave oven as well.

4 ounces very lean ground beef
2 cups chopped fresh tomato
2 cups Marinara Sauce (page 147) *or* 1 jar (14 ounces) low-sodium marinara sauce
7 ounces uncooked lasagne noodles (about 8 noodles)
2 cups farmer cheese or nonfat cottage cheese
1 cup shredded part-skim mozzarella cheese
2 tablespoons freshly grated Romano or Asiago cheese
2 tablespoons minced flat-leaf (Italian) parsley

Crumble the beef into an 11- by 7-inch microwave-proof baking dish. Cover with microwave plastic wrap, lifting a corner to vent, and microwave on high (100%) for 2 minutes.

Remove from oven and pour off the fat. Stir in the chopped tomato and Marinara Sauce, then remove about two-thirds of the mixture and set aside.

Arrange a third of the noodles over the mixture left in the bottom of the dish and top with another third of the mixture. Arrange another third of the noodles over it, then spread with half of the farmer cheese. Repeat, using the remaining noodles, cheese, and sauce. Cover with a double layer of microwave plastic wrap and lift back one corner to vent. Microwave on high (100%) for 15 minutes, rotating the dish once if necessary. Reduce the power to medium (50%) and cook until the noodles are tender (12 to 15 minutes).

Pull back the plastic wrap, then sprinkle the mozzarella and Romano over the top. Cover and let stand until the cheese is melted (about 10 minutes). Sprinkle with the parsley and serve.

Serves 6.

Meat Loaf with Italian Filling

This meat loaf has a hidden filling of cheeses and zucchini. Serve it with herbed rice or potatoes, crusty whole-grain French bread, and hearty Italian red wine.

1 pound lean ground beef
4 ounces turkey pepperoni, chopped fine
3/4 cup whole wheat or Italian-style bread crumbs
1 cup Tomato Sauce (page 147)
1/2 cup grated onion
1/2 teaspoon salt
1/4 teaspoon freshly ground black pepper
2 teaspoons dried oregano or Italian Herb Blend (page 150)
2 eggs
3/4 cup nonfat cottage cheese, drained, or farmer cheese
1/4 cup grated Parmesan cheese
1 cup shredded zucchini
1/4 cup chopped flat-leaf (Italian) parsley

In a large bowl combine the beef, pepperoni, bread crumbs, Tomato Sauce, onion, salt, ground pepper, oregano, and one of the eggs. In a medium bowl combine the other egg with the cottage cheese, Parmesan, zucchini, and parsley.

Press half of the meat mixture into a large loaf pan. Make a shallow groove lengthwise down the center and spoon the cheese mixture into it. Cover with the remaining meat mixture and pat firmly at the sides and corners.

Bake at 350 degrees F for about 1 hour. Let stand for 10 minutes before serving.

Serves 6 to 8.

Summer Garden Meat Loaf

This faintly Italian-style meat loaf uses fresh garden vegetables. With a mixed green salad, it makes a perfect late summer meal.

1/2 pound lean ground beef
1/2 pound freshly ground uncooked turkey
2 egg whites
3/4 cup quick-cooking rolled oats
3/4 cup skim milk or Vegetable Stock (page 147)
4 small new potatoes (about 1/2 pound), sliced very thin
1/2 cup shredded carrot
1/2 cup shredded zucchini
1/4 cup finely chopped green bell pepper
1/4 cup finely chopped onion
1/2 teaspoon dry mustard
2 teaspoons Worcestershire sauce
1/4 teaspoon salt
1/4 teaspoon dried marjoram
1/4 teaspoon freshly ground black pepper
2 tablespoons grated Parmesan cheese
1 tablespoon low-sodium soy sauce
1 pound plum tomatoes (about 2 cups), skins removed, halved lengthwise, or 1 can (16 ounces) plum tomatoes, drained and halved

In a large bowl combine all but the last three ingredients. Shape the mixture into a loaf about 9 by 5 inches, and place in a shallow roasting pan. Bake at 350 degrees F for 30 minutes.

Remove from the oven and sprinkle the cheese over the top. Drizzle the soy sauce over the tomato halves. Place them in overlapping rows on top of the loaf. Bake for 45 minutes; let stand for 5 minutes before slicing.

Serves 6.

Norwegian Lamb and Cabbage

This easy dish, traditional fare for a Norwegian family, is served right from the pot. Use the leanest lamb you can find; if possible, have a butcher bone it for you and ask for the bones. While the stew simmers in the oven, the cook can relax. Start off this meal with a warm fruit soup and serve the lamb and cabbage with hearty rye bread. The traditional Norwegian dessert would be a delicate rice pudding into which one whole almond is baked. Whoever gets it receives a special gift.

2 pounds lamb, with bones, all visible fat removed
1 head cabbage (3 pounds), cored
Salt, to taste
6 small potatoes, sliced thin
All-purpose flour, as needed
6 peppercorns
1/2 cup water, or more as needed

Cut the meat into chunks and the cabbage into thick slices; set aside.

In a large flameproof Dutch oven over medium heat, brown the bones. Remove them and pour off any fat. Arrange a layer of meat on the bottom of the pot and sprinkle with a little salt. Add a layer each of cabbage and potatoes. Roll the remaining meat in a little flour and repeat the layers (with a little salt on each layer of meat), ending with potatoes.

Either put the peppercorns in a bag in the middle or sprinkle throughout (they lose their bite in the cooking). Pour the water over the top, cover the pot, and cook in a 300 degree F oven for about 2 1/2 hours, adding more water if necessary. If you want to brown the potatoes on top, uncover the pot, increase the heat to 350 degrees F, and cook for about 20 minutes longer. Serve hot.

Serves 6 to 8.

Shepherd's Pie

Here is an adaptation of traditional British fare. Back in earlier days the pie would have had flour mixed with the potatoes, not to mention a generous amount of drippings or lard. Since few of us today need that extra fat while tending the sheep, we'll settle for this leaner dish.

2 large potatoes, peeled and cut into small pieces
1/4 cup skim milk
2 teaspoons light margarine
Dash salt
3/4 pound lean ground lamb
1 1/2 cups chopped onion
1/2 cups chopped celery
1/2 cup chopped carrot
2 tablespoons all-purpose flour
1 cup water or Vegetable Stock (page 147)
3 tablespoons Crushed Tomatoes (page 148) or tomato paste
1 teaspoon ground marjoram
1/2 teaspoon ground thyme
1/4 teaspoon salt
1/4 teaspoon freshly ground black pepper
1 cup frozen peas
1/2 cup frozen green beans

Cook the potato pieces in boiling water until very tender. Drain and mash with the milk, margarine, and salt. Set aside.

In a large Dutch oven over medium heat, brown the lamb, onion, celery, and carrot, breaking up the meat with a fork. Drain off any excess fat and pat dry.

Stir in the flour, then add the water, tomatoes, marjoram, thyme, salt, and ground pepper. Cook, stirring, until the mixture thickens. Reduce the heat, mix in the frozen vegetables, cover, and cook for about 5 minutes.

Spoon the reserved mashed potatoes over the top, spreading to cover. Run a fork over the top to make a crisscross pattern. Bake at 350 degrees F until the potatoes are lightly browned (about 35 minutes). Serve hot.

Serves 4.

Variations

Turkey Vegetable Pie. Substitute ground turkey for the lamb and rubbed dried sage for the marjoram.

Old-fashioned Meat Pie. Boil the potatoes instead of mashing them. Drain and add them with the frozen vegetables. Top the pie with Triple Wheat Biscuits (page 152) and bake at 425 degrees F for about 20 minutes.

Navarin d'Agneau

Probably one of the most popular French country dishes, this savory stew can be made with leftover lamb from a roast. Do include the turnips, the ingredient that makes the recipe authentic. Serve this with a mixed green salad and crusty whole-grain French bread.

1 tablespoon vegetable oil
1 medium onion, chopped
2 large cloves garlic, pressed or minced
2 pounds lean lamb, cut into 1 1/2-inch cubes
2 tablespoons Crushed Tomatoes (page 148) or tomato paste
1 cup Beef Stock (page 146)
1/2 cup chopped parsley
1/2 teaspoon salt
1/4 teaspoon freshly ground black pepper
1 teaspoon fresh oregano leaves *or* 1/2 teaspoon dried oregano
1/2 teaspoon dried basil
1 cup dry white wine
1 teaspoon butter or light margarine
6 medium carrots, cut into 1-inch chunks
4 turnips (about 1 pound), scraped and cut into 1-inch chunks
16 small boiling onions
1 1/2 pounds small potatoes, sliced
2 teaspoons cornstarch dissolved in 2 teaspoons water (optional)

In a large skillet over medium heat, warm the oil. Sauté the onion and garlic until the onion is soft. Transfer to a 3-quart casserole.

Add the lamb cubes to the pan and brown lightly on all sides. Mix with the onion and garlic in the casserole. Pour off any excess fat from the pan. Add the tomatoes, stock, parsley, salt, ground pepper, oregano, and basil; bring to a boil, scraping up the browned bits. Pour over the lamb along with the wine. Cover the casserole and bake at 325 degrees F for 1 hour.

In the same pan melt the butter over medium heat; add the carrots, turnips, onions, and potatoes. Cook quickly, stirring, until the vegetables are glazed and lightly browned. Add them to the lamb and bake until the lamb and vegetables are tender (about 1 hour). If desired, cook the cornstarch mixture until clear and use it to thicken the sauce. Serve the stew piping hot.

Serves 8.

Variation

Austrian Lamb Stew. Omit the garlic. Substitute 1/2 teaspoon caraway seeds for the oregano and basil. Substitute 1 cup cauliflower florets and 1 cup diced peeled tomato for the turnips.

Armenian Lamb Stew

Lamb is one of the basic foods of the Mediterranean, Central Europe, and the Middle East. Here is one of many preparations. Serve it with warm pita bread and a green salad tossed with fresh mint, Greek olives, and Yogurt Herb Topping (page 150).

1 1/2 cups long-grain white rice
Boiling water, as needed
1 tablespoon olive oil, or more as needed
4 cloves garlic, minced
2 pounds lean lamb, cut into bite-sized pieces
1 quart home-processed tomatoes *or* 2 cans (16 ounces each) unsalted tomatoes
1 can (6 ounces) tomato paste
1 teaspoon salt
1 teaspoon dried oregano
1/2 teaspoon freshly ground black pepper
1 large eggplant, cut into 1/2-inch cubes
4 yellow summer squash, sliced
2 large green bell peppers, halved, seeded, and cut into strips

Measure the rice into a large bowl and cover with the boiling water. Let the rice soak while you prepare the casserole.

In a large Dutch oven with a tight-fitting lid, warm the oil over medium heat. Add the garlic and lamb pieces and cook until browned. Remove the lamb and garlic to a platter and drain off any excess fat.

Drain the tomatoes, reserving the liquid. Blend the tomato paste with the reserved liquid and set aside. Break the tomatoes into pieces and spread half of them over the bottom of a casserole dish. Combine the salt, oregano, and ground pepper; sprinkle a little over the tomatoes. Make layers of half the eggplant, squash, bell peppers, and reserved lamb, sprinkling each layer with seasoning. Repeat the layers. Drain the rice and spread it on top. Then spoon the reserved tomato liquid over the top and drizzle a small amount of olive oil over all.

Cover and bake at 325 degrees F for about 1 1/2 hours, adding a little boiling water if necessary. Remove the lid and bake for 10 minutes longer. Serve hot.

Serves 8.

Pork Chops with Sauerkraut, German Style

This is but one version of a popular Central European dish that comes in many forms, all easy and very hearty. If possible, use refrigerated sauerkraut packaged in plastic bags, since it is less salty and crisper than canned. Serve this dish with a mixed green salad and cold beer.

4 strips turkey bacon
8 thin loin pork chops (about 3/4 inch thick), all
  visible fat removed
1 medium onion, sliced thin
1 quart sauerkraut, drained and rinsed
1 large tart apple, diced
1 teaspoon caraway seeds
1/2 cup dry white wine
2 large potatoes, sliced very thin

In a large skillet over medium heat, fry the bacon until crisp. Drain, crumble, and set aside.

Drain off the fat from the skillet, increase the heat to medium-high, and quickly sauté the chops and onion until browned. Arrange them in a 14- by 10-inch baking dish or a large shallow round casserole with a lid.

Wipe most of the fat from the skillet and turn the sauerkraut into the pan. Stir in the apple and caraway seeds and brown slightly. Remove from the heat and stir in the white wine and reserved bacon.

Spread half of the sauerkraut mixture over the chops, then arrange the sliced potatoes over it. Cover with the remaining sauerkraut mixture. Cover the dish with aluminum foil and bake at 350 degrees F for 30 minutes. Uncover and continue baking until the potatoes are done and the sauerkraut is slightly glazed (about 15 minutes). Serve hot.

Serves 4.

Variation

Sausages with Sauerkraut. Substitute 1 to 1 1/2 pounds kielbasa, knockwurst, or other fully cooked sausage (preferably turkey sausage) for the pork chops and bacon. Brown them in the skillet as you would the bacon. Remove from the pan, drain, and score diagonally. Pour off almost all the fat and prepare the sauerkraut mixture as above. Layer it and the potatoes in the casserole first and arrange the sausages on top. Bake as above. Serves 4 to 6.

Pork Chops and Carrots, English Style

This delicious combination of pork and vegetables with herbs represents the very best of British country cooking. Serve it with crusty light rye bread and crisp dry white wine.

8 medium carrots, halved crosswise, then quartered lengthwise
1/4 cup all-purpose flour
1 teaspoon rubbed dried sage
1/2 teaspoon dried thyme
1/2 teaspoon salt
1/4 teaspoon freshly ground white pepper
8 thin-cut loin pork chops, all visible fat removed
4 small potatoes (about 1/2 pound), sliced very thin
1 large onion, sliced very thin
1 medium tart apple, unpeeled and sliced very thin
1/3 cup water or Beef Stock (page 146)

Arrange the carrot pieces in the bottom of a 14-by 10-inch baking dish.

Combine the flour, sage, thyme, salt, and ground pepper in a paper bag. Shake the chops, one at a time, in the seasoned flour, then place them in the pan on top of the carrots. Arrange the potatoes, onion, and apple slices on top of the pork chops.

Cover the dish with aluminum foil and bake at 350 degrees F until the meat and vegetables are done (about 50 minutes). Serve hot.

Serves 4 to 6.

Pork and Kumara Casserole

This New Zealand dish features the sweet potato, known there as *kumara*, brought by Maori settlers and used in cooking since the seventh or eighth century. That's food with a tradition!

1 cup (8 ounces) lean pork pieces, all visible fat removed
1 large sweet potato, peeled and cubed
2 medium onions, chopped
2 tablespoons all-purpose flour
1 cup unsweetened pineapple juice
2 tablespoons distilled white vinegar
2 tablespoons low-sodium soy sauce
2 tablespoons dry sherry
2 cups peas, fresh or frozen
1 cup pineapple chunks, drained

Place the pork, sweet potato, and onions in a casserole dish. Mix the flour with the pineapple juice, vinegar, soy sauce, and sherry; pour over the pork mixture.

Cover the casserole and cook at 350 degrees F for 1 1/2 hours, stirring occasionally. Add the peas and pineapple and cook, uncovered, for 10 minutes longer. Serve hot.

Serves 4.

Pork Stew with Peppers and Mushrooms

This oven dish has been a favorite in my home for years. It is easy to make and can be prepared with many different accompaniments. This is the basic dish, really an English braised meat style of dinner. Some suggested variations follow. The stew is excellent served with thick slices of dark rye bread and mugs of chilled beer.

2 pounds pork tenderloin, all visible fat removed, cut into pieces
1/2 cup water
2 large onions, sliced
4 medium potatoes, halved and sliced
3 carrots, cut into thirds crosswise, then quartered lengthwise
1 bay leaf
1 teaspoon dried winter savory
1/2 teaspoon salt
1/2 teaspoon freshly ground white pepper
1/4 pound fresh mushrooms, sliced
1 cup sliced zucchini
1 large green bell pepper, sliced
1/2 large red bell pepper, sliced

In a heavy Dutch oven over medium heat, brown the pork pieces. Add the water, onions, potatoes, carrots, bay leaf, savory, salt, and ground pepper. Cover and bake in a 300 degree F oven for 2 hours.

Add the mushrooms, zucchini, and bell pepper slices. Cover and cook for 1 hour longer. Discard the bay leaf. Serve hot.

Serves 6 to 8.

Variations

For both variations, omit the carrots, mushrooms, zucchini, bay leaf, and savory.

Yugoslav Pork with String Beans. Brown the onions and bell peppers with the pork. Add 1 teaspoon paprika. After the stew has cooked for 2 hours, add 1 pound fresh or frozen green beans, cut into pieces. Thicken the sauce with 1 tablespoon flour mixed with 1/4 cup water; add more paprika to taste. Garnish with plain low-fat yogurt.

Mexican Pork with Chile Verde. Cut the pork into 2-inch cubes, chop the onions, and cube the potatoes; brown them in a small amount of vegetable oil over medium heat. In a blender combine 3 cloves garlic; 1/4 cup chopped cilantro; 3 tomatillos; and 2 fresh jalapeño peppers, membranes and seeds removed, *or* 1 can (8 ounces) green chiles. Pour the sauce over the meat mixture, add 1 cup chopped tomato, and substitute 1/2 cup tomato juice for the water. Cover and cook in the oven until the pork is done (at least 1 hour). Add water if needed. The stew should be rather thick. Serve with warm flour tortillas.

Pork and Rice, Spanish Style

This dish has many variations, but I like this one especially because of the healthful combination of chick-peas and brown rice to go along with the pork.

1 tablespoon olive oil
1 pound lean boneless pork, cubed
1 cup chopped onion
3 cloves garlic, minced
1 cup diced green bell pepper
1 cup long-grain brown rice
1 cup hot water
1 can (28 ounces) whole tomatoes, chopped, with juice
1/2 cup dry red wine
1/2 teaspoon salt
1/2 teaspoon freshly ground black pepper
2 bay leaves
1 1/2 pounds young summer squash, sliced
1 1/2 cups cooked chick-peas, drained

In a heavy Dutch oven over medium heat, warm the olive oil. Lightly brown the pork, onion, garlic, and bell pepper. Stir in the rice and brown for several minutes. Then add the hot water, tomatoes, wine, salt, ground pepper, and bay leaves.

Cover the pot and bake in a 350 degree F oven for 1 hour, stirring occasionally. Stir in the summer squash and chick-peas and bake for about 30 minutes longer. Remove the bay leaves, taste, and adjust the seasonings. Add more liquid if the stew seems too dry. Serve hot.

Serves 8.

Variation

Pork and Rice, Hungarian Style. Add 1 tablespoon sweet Hungarian paprika when browning the pork. Substitute 1 tablespoon caraway seeds for the bay leaves and 2 cups shredded cabbage for the summer squash. Just before serving stir in 1 cup plain low-fat yogurt. Heat thoroughly but do not boil.

Crustless Ham and Green Vegetable Pie

Here is a slimmed-down version of Italian-style spinach and ricotta tart and its close relative the French quiche. By eliminating the crust (sadly enough, a tender, flaky place where much fat lurks) and by using farmer cheese, you can achieve a delicious lean alternative. With a salad of tomatoes and mixed greens and a loaf of warm, crusty whole-grain French bread, you have a complete supper.

1 tablespoon olive oil
1/4 pound fresh mushrooms, sliced
1 green bell pepper, diced
1 medium zucchini, diced
2 large green onions, minced
1/2 cup diced ham (preferably turkey ham)
1 cup shredded part-skim mozzarella cheese
8 ounces farmer cheese
8 ounces reduced-fat ricotta cheese
2 large eggs *or* 1/2 cup egg substitute
1 cup chopped spinach
1 teaspoon dried dill weed
1/2 teaspoon salt
1/2 teaspoon freshly ground white pepper
1 egg white, beaten until stiff
Vegetable spray, for baking dish

In a medium skillet over medium heat, warm the oil. Sauté the mushrooms, bell pepper, zucchini, and green onions until slightly tender. Stir in the ham and set aside to cool.

Measure the cheeses into a 4-cup measure and beat in the eggs. Add to the ham mixture along with the spinach, dill, salt, and ground pepper. Gently fold in the egg white.

Spray an 11- by 9-inch baking dish with vegetable spray (or lightly oil the dish). Pour in the mixture and bake at 350 degrees F until set (about 45 minutes). Serve hot.

Serves 6.

Variation
Beer and Cheese Vegetable Pie. Omit the salt. Spread 8 slices dry whole wheat bread with 1 tablespoon country-style or Dijon mustard and cut into 1-inch cubes. Combine with the vegetables, ham, cheese, and eggs and let stand for 15 minutes. Stir in 1/2 cup beer and fold in the egg white. Bake at 350 degrees F until puffed and golden brown (about 45 minutes).

Poulet en Cocotte

A dish that creates its own sauce, this is a delicious and easy way to prepare a whole chicken. Remove the skin before carving the chicken. Serve with crusty French bread and a salad of soft head lettuce (such as Boston) and tiny barely cooked peas with Light Herb Dressing (page 149).

1 1/2 cups sliced leek, white part only
1 medium zucchini, cut into 1/4-inch slices
2 large green bell peppers, cut into 1/4-inch strips
1 large red bell pepper, cut into 1/4-inch strips
4 cups thinly sliced small red potato
1/2 cup boiling water
2 teaspoons finely crushed dried thyme
1/2 teaspoon salt
1/3 cup dry white wine
1 roasting chicken (about 3 pounds)
Juice of 1/2 small lemon
1 small bunch parsley
1 cup leek pieces, green part only

Arrange the sliced leek, zucchini, pepper strips, and potato in the bottom of a covered Dutch oven or roaster large enough to hold the chicken. Pour the boiling water over the vegetables. Mix the thyme and salt together and sprinkle half of it on top. Pour the wine over all.

Rinse the chicken and pat dry. Squeeze the lemon into the cavity and rub in the juice. Place the parsley and green part of the leek in the cavity. Sprinkle the remaining thyme mixture over the chicken and place the chicken on top of the vegetables.

Cover the pot and bake the chicken at 325 degrees F until it is tender (about 2 hours). Transfer the chicken to a platter; remove and discard the parsley and leek from the cavity. Surround the chicken with the vegetables; slice the chicken and discard the skin. Serve piping hot.

Serves 4 to 6.

Variations

Poulet en Cocotte Bonne Femme. Sauté 2 slices bacon in the Dutch oven until crisp. Blot on a paper towel and drain any excess fat from the pot. Use 1 green bell pepper and add 10 small white onions. Crumble the bacon over the chicken before baking.

Sesame Tarragon Chicken. Substitute dried tarragon for the thyme and sprinkle 2 tablespoons sesame seeds over the chicken. After the chicken has baked for 1 hour, combine some of the sauce with 1/2 cup plain low-fat yogurt and pour over the chicken and vegetables. Continue cooking as above. After you slice the chicken, garnish the dish with 3 tablespoons toasted sesame seeds.

Chicken and Spaghetti with Bell Peppers

Although somewhat similar to the stove-top Chicken Cacciatore (page 82), this dish goes into the oven and the spaghetti cooks right along with everything else. Serve it with a salad of fresh mixed greens with Creamy Vinaigrette (page 149) and Simple Garlic Bread (page 152) to soak up the sauce.

1 tablespoon vegetable oil
1 broiler-fryer chicken (about 3 pounds), cut into parts and skinned
1 medium onion, chopped
1 large clove garlic, minced
1/4 pound fresh mushrooms, sliced
1 1/2 cups water
2 cups Tomato Sauce (page 147)
1 teaspoon Italian Herb Blend (page 150)
1/2 teaspoon salt
1/2 teaspoon freshly ground black pepper
4 ounces spaghetti, broken (about 1 1/2 cups)
1 medium zucchini, sliced
1 medium green bell pepper, halved and sliced
Grated Parmesan cheese, for sprinkling

In a large Dutch oven over medium heat, warm the oil. Brown the chicken parts, then add the onion, garlic, and mushrooms and sauté until the onion is tender. Stir in the water, Tomato Sauce, herb blend, salt, and ground pepper. Cover and bake at 350 degrees F for 30 minutes.

Stir in the spaghetti, zucchini, and bell pepper. Cover and bake until the chicken and spaghetti are tender (about 30 minutes), stirring occasionally. Sprinkle with the grated Parmesan and serve.

Serves 4 to 6.

Microwave Variation

Heat the oil in a 3-quart round casserole, uncovered, for 2 minutes on high (100%). Add the onion, garlic, and mushrooms, stir to coat, and cook, uncovered, for 2 minutes on high. Stir in 3/4 cup water, the Tomato Sauce, and the seasonings. Mound the vegetables in the center and arrange the chicken pieces around them, breasts in the center, smaller pieces around the edges. Cover tightly with microwave plastic wrap and cook for 15 minutes on high.

Peel back the wrap and stir in the spaghetti and vegetables. Cover again and microwave on high until the chicken and spaghetti are tender (15 minutes).

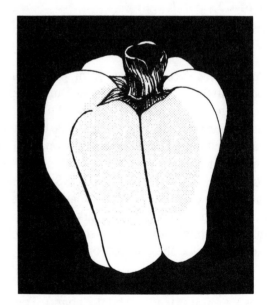

Chicken Pot Pie, Chilean Style

This is an adaptation of a popular Chilean dish called *Pastel de choclo*, which is topped with corn rather than pastry. A touch of sugar on top melts into a thin golden skin.

2 tablespoons light margarine
1 medium onion, chopped
1 clove garlic, minced
2 tablespoons all-purpose flour
2 cups Chicken Stock (page 146), hot
1/2 teaspoon paprika
1/2 teaspoon ground cumin
1/4 teaspoon cayenne pepper
3 large tomatoes, peeled, seeded, and chopped
1 green bell pepper, halved and cut into strips
1 large carrot, cut into thin rounds
3 cups cooked chicken pieces (bite-sized)
1/2 cup pitted ripe olives
1/4 cup sliced almonds
1/4 cup raisins
1 can (16 1/2 ounces) cream-style corn
4 teaspoons sugar

In a large skillet over medium heat, melt the margarine. Add the onion and garlic and sauté until the onion is soft. Blend in 1 tablespoon of the flour and cook, stirring, until bubbly. Gradually pour in the stock and continue cooking, stirring, until the sauce boils and thickens. Stir in the paprika, cumin, cayenne, tomatoes, bell pepper, and carrot. Simmer for 5 minutes.

Remove the pan from the heat and stir in the chicken, olives, almonds, and raisins. Pour the mixture into a shallow 2-quart casserole or an 11- by 9-inch baking dish.

Wipe the pan clean, heat the remaining 1 tablespoon flour, and add the corn. Cook, stirring, until thickened. Spoon over the top of the casserole, then sprinkle with the sugar. Bake at 350 degrees F for 35 minutes, then place under the broiler until the top is golden brown (about 5 minutes). Serve at once.

Serves 6.

Variation

Mexican Chicken Pot Pie. Omit the carrot, almonds, and raisins. Drain the creamed corn and stir it into the chicken mixture. Cover the pie with a cornmeal topping made by scalding 1 1/2 cups skim milk with 1/4 teaspoon salt and 1 tablespoon light margarine. Gradually stir in 1 cup cornmeal and cook, stirring, until thickened. Remove from the heat and stir in 1/2 cup shredded reduced-fat Cheddar or Monterey jack cheese. Spread over the casserole and bake at 375 degrees F until lightly browned (about 30 minutes). Serve with Dick's Salsa (page 149) or Green Chile Salsa (page 149).

Dijon Chicken and Vegetables

Here is a very easy chicken meal, and one that can be quickly made in the microwave. This dish is good with an apple salad on greens with Orange Ginger Dressing (page 150).

1 medium onion, sliced
1 medium carrot, sliced thin
1 cup cut-up broccoli
1 cup sliced zucchini
1 cup thinly sliced potato
1 broiler-fryer chicken (about 3 pounds), cut into parts and skinned
3 tablespoons Dijon mustard
2 tablespoons light margarine, melted

Arrange the onion, carrot, broccoli, zucchini, and potato evenly over the bottom of a 13- by 9-inch baking dish. Place the chicken parts on top of the vegetables. Combine the mustard and melted margarine and brush it over the chicken.

Cover the dish with aluminum foil and bake at 350 degrees F until the chicken is tender (about 1 hour). Serve hot.

Serves 4 to 6.

Microwave Variation

Use a total of 2 cups vegetables, other possibilities being celery, tomatoes, green bell peppers, cauliflower, and green beans. Use a 2-quart microwave-proof dish and arrange the chicken with breast halves in the center and legs (bone end pointing toward the center), thighs, wings, and backs around them. Cover tightly with microwave plastic wrap. Microwave on high (100%) for 18 to 22 minutes, rotating the dish if necessary. The chicken is done when a fork can be inserted with ease. Serves 4.

Italian Zucchini and Rice Bake

I have made this casserole more often than any other in my cooking career. Serve it with a salad of mixed greens, topped with Light Herb Dressing (page 149), and light Italian red wine.

1 teaspoon olive oil
1/2 cup chopped onion
1 large clove garlic, minced
1/2 teaspoon salt
1/4 teaspoon freshly ground black pepper
1/2 teaspoon dried basil
3/4 cup chopped cooked chicken or turkey
1 1/2 cups cooked brown rice
1/2 cup Tomato Sauce (page 147)
1 egg
1/2 cup nonfat cottage cheese
1/4 cup chopped parsley, preferably flat-leaf
3 cups thinly sliced small zucchini
1/2 cup shredded reduced-fat Cheddar cheese

In a large skillet over medium heat, warm the oil. Sauté the onion, garlic, salt, ground pepper, and basil until the onion is transparent. Stir in the chicken, rice, and Tomato Sauce. Set aside.

Beat the egg into the cottage cheese, then stir in the parsley. Arrange half the zucchini slices in a 6-cup casserole or an 11- by 9-inch baking dish. Spoon the rice mixture over the top, then spread the cottage cheese mixture over all. Top with the remaining zucchini slices and sprinkle with the shredded cheese. Bake at 350 degrees F until the casserole is bubbly and the cheese nicely browned (40 to 45 minutes). Serve immediately.

Serves 4 to 6.

Chicken Tetrazzini

As the story goes, this dish was named for Luisa Tetrazzini, a soprano noted for her brilliant coloratura technique and her rather large girth. The recipe in its original form suited her size. This one is a lot slimmer. Serve with a salad of sliced apples and raisins on a bed of greens with Orange Ginger Dressing (page 150).

1 package (7 ounces) thin spaghetti, broken into
    4-inch pieces
1 tablespoon olive oil
3 cups sliced fresh mushrooms
1/2 cup finely chopped onion
1 small green bell pepper, cut into small strips
1/2 small red bell pepper, cut into small strips
3 tablespoons all-purpose flour
1 cup skim milk
1 cup evaporated skimmed milk
1/4 cup dry sherry
1/2 teaspoon salt
1/2 teaspoon freshly ground white pepper
2 cups chopped cooked chicken breast
1 cup frozen tiny peas, defrosted
2 tablespoons grated Parmesan cheese

Cook the spaghetti according to directions on page 46; drain well. Arrange the cooked spaghetti in a shallow rectangular baking dish or 3-quart casserole; set aside.

In a large skillet over medium heat, warm the oil. Sauté the mushrooms, onion, and bell peppers until the vegetables are slightly softened. Stir in the flour and gradually add the skim milk and evaporated milk. Bring to a boil, stirring constantly, and cook for 5 minutes. Remove from the heat and stir in the sherry, salt, ground pepper, chicken, and peas.

Pour the chicken mixture over the reserved spaghetti and sprinkle with the cheese. Bake at 300 degrees F for about 45 minutes, then place under the broiler until browned. Serve hot.

Serves 6.

Variations

Microwave Variation. Omit the baking step; instead, cover with microwave plastic wrap and microwave on medium-high (70%) until thoroughly heated (15 to 18 minutes). Brown under the broiler, if desired.

Turkey Tetrazzini. Substitute 2 cups chopped cooked turkey (white meat) for the chicken.

Chicken Enchiladas

In this adaptation of the popular enchilada, the tortillas are layered rather than rolled around the filling, for a meal that is quicker, easier, and different. These go well with salsa and well-chilled beer.

1 teaspoon canola oil
1 cup chopped onion
2 large cloves garlic, minced
1 teaspoon ground cumin, plus dash cumin
1 teaspoon chili powder
1 cup chopped cooked chicken
2 cups cooked red kidney beans *or* 1 can (15 ounces) red kidney beans, rinsed and drained
1 cup Tomato Sauce (page 147) *or* 1 can (8 ounces) no-salt tomato sauce
1 can (4 ounces) chopped green chiles, drained
2 cups nonfat cottage cheese
1 egg white, lightly beaten
9 corn tortillas (6-inch size), cut in half
1 cup shredded reduced-fat Monterey jack cheese
1/2 cup plain nonfat yogurt
1 cup coarsely shredded lettuce
1 cup chopped ripe tomato
Dick's Salsa (page 149) or Green Chile Salsa (page 149)

In a nonstick skillet over medium-high heat, warm the oil. Sauté the onion and garlic until the onion is soft. Stir in the 1 teaspoon cumin, chili powder, chopped chicken, kidney beans, Tomato Sauce, and chiles. Mix well and set aside.

Measure the cottage cheese into a 4-cup measure and beat in the egg white. Set aside.

Arrange 6 tortilla halves in the bottom of a 3-quart casserole; spread with a third of the chicken mixture, then a third of the cottage cheese mixture.

Top with 1/3 cup shredded cheese. Repeat the layers twice, ending with the cheese.

Bake at 350 degrees F until thoroughly heated (about 45 minutes). Let stand for 5 minutes. Stir the dash cumin into the yogurt. Serve the enchiladas topped with the lettuce, tomato, and yogurt-cumin combination. Pass the salsa on the side.

Serves 4 to 6.

Microwave Variation

Instead of baking the casserole, cover it loosely with microwave plastic wrap and microwave on medium-high (70%) until the center is thoroughly heated (about 10 minutes).

Turkey Pot Pie

Meat pie has been a staple of British cooking for centuries. Here is an adaptation of the old-fashioned and traditional American version, without the bottom pastry crust and with biscuit topping. This is a wonderful way to enjoy leftover turkey. Serve it with an apple and raisin salad on a bed of greens with Orange Ginger Dressing (page 150) and hearty whole wheat bread.

3 tablespoons light margarine
1/2 cup sliced celery
1/2 cup chopped green bell pepper
1 cup chopped onion
1 cup thinly sliced carrot
1/3 cup all-purpose flour
2 3/4 cups Chicken Stock (page 146) or Turkey
  Stock (page 146)
1/2 teaspoon salt
1/2 teaspoon dried thyme
1/2 teaspoon dried rosemary
1/2 teaspoon dried tarragon
1/2 teaspoon dried sage
1/4 teaspoon freshly ground black pepper
1/4 cup dry sherry
3 cups cubed cooked turkey
1 cup frozen tiny peas, defrosted
Triple Wheat Biscuits (page 152)

In a large skillet over medium heat, melt the margarine. Sauté the celery, bell pepper, onion, and carrot until the vegetables are slightly soft. Sprinkle with the flour and blend. Gradually add the stock and cook, stirring constantly, until the sauce comes to a boil and thickens. Remove from the heat and stir in the salt, thyme, rosemary, tarragon, sage, ground pepper, sherry, turkey, and peas. Spoon into a 3-quart baking dish.

Prepare the biscuit dough and arrange on top of the turkey-vegetable mixture in the casserole, leaving space between the biscuits for steam to escape. (Extra biscuits can be baked separately on a baking sheet.) Bake in a 425 degree F oven until the biscuits are golden brown (20 to 25 minutes). Serve hot.

Serves 8.

Variation
Chicken Pot Pie. Use Chicken Stock. Add 1/2 cup cubed zucchini to the sautéed vegetables and substitute cubed cooked chicken for the turkey.

Turkey and Wild Rice Casserole

Wild rice comes from the northern United States and is grown today mostly in northern Minnesota. It is not rice at all but the kernel from an aquatic wild grass that has long played an important role in the life of American Indians, especially the Ojibway tribe. This dish is an adaptation of an Ojibway casserole, which might well have contained wild game or fowl rather than turkey. A traditional accompaniment would be fried bread or a biscuitlike bread called bannock, and preserves made from berries and sweetened with maple syrup.

1/2 cup uncooked wild rice
1/2 cup uncooked long-grain white rice
2 1/4 cups Chicken Stock (page 146), or more as needed
1 cup finely chopped onion
3/4 cup sliced celery
1/2 teaspoon salt
1/4 teaspoon freshly ground black pepper
3 cups sliced fresh mushrooms
1 cup fresh or frozen peas
1/4 cup chopped parsley
1/2 teaspoon dried rosemary, crushed
3 cups cubed cooked turkey

In a 3-quart casserole with a lid, combine the rices, stock, onion, celery, salt, and ground pepper. Cover and bake at 350 degrees F for 1 1/4 hours (see Note).

Remove the casserole from the oven and gently stir in the mushrooms, peas, parsley, rosemary, and turkey. Cover and bake until the rice is tender (about 30 minutes). Serve hot.

Serves 6.

Note: Because wild rice varies in moisture, check the casserole after the first 45 minutes to make sure that there is enough liquid. Add water or more stock if it is too dry.

Variation

Turkey, Artichoke, and Wild Rice Casserole. Substitute 1 package (9 ounces) frozen artichoke hearts, defrosted and halved, for the peas, and stir in 1/4 cup dry sherry.

Turkey Sausage, Zucchini, and Mushroom Pizza

Despite some assertions that this universally popular food is of American origin, pizza comes from Italy and probably originated in Naples, where hungry peasants used to break off pieces of bread while it was baking, flatten the dough, and top it with whatever seasonings were at hand. Tomatoes were not added at the beginning (they were thought to be poisonous) and cheese wasn't even considered until the end of the nineteenth century.

This simple dish put on weight when it came to America. Laden with cheese and meat, it has become, along with the hamburger, the favorite of fast foods. But any visit to the pizza parlor will show you that variety is the name of the game. Using that variety while thinking lean can create some interesting dishes. Pizza is one of those wonderful, quick-cooking complete meals; add a mixed green salad and beverage and your dinner is ready.

Pizza has two basic parts, the crust and the toppings. Make a whole wheat crust and add herbs, if desired; or try a crust of rice (page 43). The toppings can be almost anything you choose, especially vegetable combinations. Try various cheeses and use less of them. Try a creamy sauce or an Asian brown bean sauce instead of cheese. And instead of pork sausage with lots of fat, try turkey sausage.

6 ounces Italian-flavored bulk turkey sausage
4 cups finely sliced fresh mushrooms (about 12 ounces mushrooms)
1/2 cup chopped onion
6 large cloves garlic, minced
1/4 cup evaporated skimmed milk
3 tablespoons chopped parsley
1/2 cup (2 ounces) shredded provolone cheese
1 Whole Wheat Pizza Dough (page 151)
2 cups thinly sliced small zucchini
1/4 cup grated fresh Romano cheese

In a large skillet over medium heat, cook the sausage until browned, stirring to crumble. Drain and pat dry with paper towels. Set aside.

Wipe out the skillet, return it to medium heat, and sauté the mushrooms, onion, and garlic for about 5 minutes. Stir in the milk and parsley and cook for an additional 2 minutes.

Sprinkle the provolone over the prepared crust. Spread the mushroom mixture evenly over the cheese, then arrange the zucchini slices and reserved sausage on top.

Sprinkle the Romano cheese over all. Bake on the bottom rack of a 500 degree F oven (or your oven's highest setting) for 12 minutes. Let stand for 5 minutes. Then cut into wedges and serve.

Serves 6.

Tuna Noodle Extraordinaire

The tuna noodle casserole has been a family staple in the States for many years. Here is an unusual version, flavored with dill and celery seeds and containing a fancy-shaped pasta (rather than noodles made with eggs) to give a traditional dish a new look. Serve with a mixed green salad and crusty whole wheat rolls.

8 ounces medium-sized fancy pasta, such as shells, ruffles, bow ties, or spirals, preferably whole wheat or vegetable pasta
1 can (6 1/2 ounces) water-packed chunk tuna, drained and flaked
1 tablespoon canola oil
1 medium onion, chopped
1 large clove garlic, minced
1/2 cup chopped celery
1/2 cup chopped green bell pepper
1/2 pound fresh mushrooms, sliced
1/2 cup sunflower seeds
1 package (10 ounces) frozen peas, defrosted
1/2 teaspoon salt
1/4 teaspoon freshly ground black pepper
1/2 teaspoon dried dill weed
1/2 teaspoon celery seeds
1 cup nonfat cottage cheese
3/4 cup plain nonfat yogurt
2 tablespoons dry sherry
1/4 cup whole wheat bread crumbs
1/4 cup shredded Cheddar cheese

Cook the pasta according to directions on page 46; rinse and drain. Combine the tuna with the drained pasta. Spread half the mixture in the bottom of a 3-quart casserole or an 11- by 7-inch baking dish. Set aside.

In a large skillet over medium heat, warm the oil. Sauté the onion, garlic, celery, bell pepper, mushrooms, and sunflower seeds until the vegetables are soft. Stir in the peas, salt, ground pepper, dill, and celery seeds. Spread half this mixture over the tuna.

In a 4-cup measure, combine the cottage cheese, yogurt, and sherry. Spoon half the mixture over the vegetable layer. Repeat the layers, ending with the cheese layer.

Combine the bread crumbs and Cheddar and sprinkle over the top of the casserole. Bake, uncovered, at 350 degrees F until the top is bubbly and lightly browned (about 30 minutes). Serve hot.

Serves 6.

Fish Fillets with Fresh Vegetables, Mediterranean Style

This dish comes in many versions, so feel free to substitute whatever fresh vegetables you have on hand. Serve with crusty French or Italian bread and crisp, dry white wine.

2 pounds fish fillets, 1/2 inch thick, such as orange roughy, red snapper, sea bass, pike, haddock, cod, or ocean perch
1 tablespoon lemon pepper
2 tablespoons olive oil
2 medium onions, sliced
3 medium carrots, sliced thin
3 stalks celery, sliced
2 leeks, sliced thin
1 clove garlic, minced
3 pounds potatoes, sliced thin
3 tomatoes, chopped *or* 1 can (15 ounces) whole tomatoes, drained and chopped
2 teaspoons snipped fresh dill weed *or* 1 teaspoon dried dill weed
1/2 teaspoon salt
1/4 cup water
1/4 cup chopped parsley
Dill sprigs, for garnish (optional)

Cut the fish into 8 serving-sized pieces. Sprinkle with the lemon pepper and set aside.

In a large skillet over medium heat, warm the oil. Add the onions, carrots, celery, leeks, garlic, and potatoes. Cook, stirring occasionally, until the vegetables are slightly tender. Stir in the tomatoes, dill, salt, and the water. Cover and simmer for 5 minutes.

Spoon about two-thirds of the vegetable mixture into the bottom of a 13- by 9-inch baking dish. Arrange the reserved fish fillets on the vegetables.

Spoon the remaining vegetables over the fish. Bake at 375 degrees F until the fish flakes easily with a fork (about 20 minutes). Garnish with the parsley and dill sprigs, if desired. Serve hot.

Serves 8.

Variation

Whitebait in Yogurt. This adaptation is from New Zealand. Use 4 cups white-fleshed fish cut into small pieces (the New Zealanders use a native trout) instead of the fillets. Substitute 1 pound steamed chopped spinach for the carrots and celery and make it the bottom layer of the casserole. Proceed as above and top the vegetables with a mixture of 1 cup plain low-fat yogurt, 1 beaten egg, 1 tablespoon dry sherry, and a pinch ground nutmeg. Sprinkle 1/4 cup shredded Cheddar cheese on top and bake as above.

Salmon Curry au Gratin, Canadian Style

Here is an easy dish, quickly assembled. A mixed green salad makes a good accompaniment.

2 tablespoons light margarine
2 tablespoons all-purpose flour
1/2 teaspoon salt
1/4 teaspoon dry mustard
2 teaspoons curry powder
1 1/2 cups skim milk
1 can (16 ounces) salmon
1/2 cup shredded reduced-fat Cheddar cheese
3 cups cooked brown rice, unsalted (1 cup
    uncooked rice)
2 cups frozen tiny peas, defrosted

In a large saucepan over medium-low heat, melt the margarine. Stir in the flour, salt, mustard, and curry; cook until bubbly. Gradually add the milk, stirring constantly, and cook until boiling and thickened.

Drain the salmon and add the liquid to the cream sauce. Remove the bones and skin from the salmon and flake it.

Add 1/4 cup of the shredded cheese to the cream sauce and stir until melted. Add the cooked rice, flaked salmon, and peas. Turn into a 3-quart casserole and sprinkle the remaining 1/4 cup shredded cheese over the top. Bake at 350 degrees F until browned and bubbly (about 30 minutes). Serve hot.

Serves 6.

Variations

Crabmeat and Broccoli Bake. Substitute 2 cups cut-up broccoli for the peas. Substitute 1 package (6 ounces) frozen crabmeat, defrosted and drained, for the salmon. Bake as above.

Curried Corn and Oysters. Substitute 1 can (16 1/2 ounces) cream-style corn for the peas. Substitute 1 pint oysters, drained and chopped coarsely, for the salmon. Stir the oysters into the hot cream sauce to cook them slightly before baking. Bake as above.

Salmon and Spinach Strata

The layers of pink salmon and green spinach in this elegant dish are lovely. Serve with a light mixed green salad with carrot slivers and Creamy Vinaigrette (page 149). Leftovers make a delicious cold snack.

1 can (16 ounces) salmon, drained, skin and bones removed
4 slices whole wheat bread, dried and crushed into coarse crumbs
1 tablespoon lime juice
1/4 cup skim milk
1 tablespoon Dijon mustard
3 tablespoons minced parsley
1 teaspoon canola oil
3 tablespoons minced shallot or green onion
1 teaspoon dried dill weed
1 package (10 ounces) fresh spinach, stems removed, leaves chopped
1/2 cup low-fat cottage cheese
1/4 teaspoon freshly ground white pepper

Break up the salmon with a fork. Mix in 1 cup bread crumbs; reserve the rest for the topping. Stir in the lime juice. Combine the milk, mustard, and parsley and stir into the salmon mixture. Set aside.

In a large saucepan over medium heat, warm the oil. Add the shallot and sauté until soft. Stir in the dill and spinach. Turn off the heat, cover, and let stand for a minute or so. Stir in the cottage cheese and ground pepper.

Spread half the salmon mixture in the bottom of an 8-inch square pan. Spread all the spinach mixture over it and top with the remaining salmon mixture. Bake at 350 degrees F for 15 minutes; spread the remaining crumbs over the top and bake until mixture is bubbly and crumbs are brown (about 10 minutes longer). Cut into rectangles to serve.

Serves 4 to 6.

Scallops and Rice, Basque Style

This dish comes from the French Pyrenees. If truly authentic, it would have *chorizo* sausage, a hot, garlicky sausage seasoned with cayenne. Instead, use garlic-flavored turkey sausage and add more cayenne if you like more heat. Frozen scallops work well here; defrost them quickly and drain before adding to the casserole. Serve this dish with tiny whole green beans topped with garlic, parsley, and lemon juice, and lots of crusty French bread.

1 cup uncooked long-grain white rice
2 cups Chicken Stock (page 146)
1 tablespoon olive oil
4 ounces spicy turkey sausage, cut into 1/4-inch pieces
1 small red bell pepper, cut into thin strips
1 small green bell pepper, cut into thin strips
1/2 teaspoon salt
1/4 teaspoon freshly ground black pepper
1/4 teaspoon cayenne pepper
1 pound scallops, rinsed and drained

In a medium-sized Dutch oven or flameproof casserole with lid, combine the rice, stock, and oil. Bring to a boil over high heat, reduce to low, and simmer, stirring frequently, for 10 minutes.

Add the sausage, bell peppers, salt, ground pepper, and cayenne and mix with a wooden spoon. Cut the scallops in half if they are small, into quarters if they are large. Add them to the casserole and mix thoroughly again. Bring to a simmer over medium heat, then immediately cover and place in a 350 degree F oven. Bake for 15 minutes, covered. Stir thoroughly, then bake uncovered, mixing lightly with a wooden spoon several times, until the liquid is absorbed and the rice is cooked (35 minutes). Serve hot.

Serves 4.

Creamy Barley with Mushrooms

It would be difficult to attribute barley to any one cooking tradition, since it has been eaten everywhere in the world since virtually the beginning of time. We usually think of it as a soup ingredient. It makes a delicious, chewy, nutty-flavored dish, high in nutrition. With this casserole serve a mixed green salad or young green beans, lightly cooked, with a light lemon-oil dressing.

1 tablespoon canola oil
2 medium onions, chopped coarsely
1 large clove garlic, minced
1 cup finely chopped celery
1 small green bell pepper, chopped
1/2 red bell pepper, chopped
1 cup pearl barley (or whole hulled barley, soaked overnight)
1 pound fresh mushrooms, sliced, divided
1 teaspoon dried thyme
1/4 teaspoon freshly ground black pepper
2 cups Vegetable Stock (page 147), divided
Salt (optional)
1/2 cup sliced almonds, toasted, divided
2 teaspoons butter or light margarine
1/4 cup minced parsley

In a flameproof casserole or Dutch oven, heat the oil over medium heat. Sauté the onions, garlic, celery, bell peppers, and barley until the onions are soft and the barley is lightly browned. Add half the mushrooms and continue cooking until they are slightly soft. Stir in the thyme and ground pepper.

Taste the stock for seasoning; if it has enough salt, there is no need to add any. Pour 1 cup of the stock over the barley and vegetables in the casserole, then stir in 1/4 cup of the almonds. Cover and bake at 350 degrees F for 30 minutes. Uncover and add the remaining 1 cup stock. Continue cooking until the liquid is absorbed and the barley is tender.

Meanwhile, sauté the remaining mushrooms in the butter and let them cook down until they are very rich, almost black. Mix in the remaining 1/4 cup almonds. Serve the casserole with this mixture spread over the top and the minced parsley sprinkled over for garnish.

Serves 4.

Zucchini and Potato Strata

With layers of vegetables and a crunchy cottage cheese-tofu filling, this casserole makes a delicious late-summer vegetarian meal. Serve it with a salad of sliced crisp apples and shredded carrot with Orange Ginger Dressing (page 150).

2 cups whole wheat bread cubes, mixed with 1/2 teaspoon Italian Herb Blend (page 150), *or* 2 cups seasoned croutons
1 cup nonfat cottage cheese
1 cup crumbled soft tofu
1 tablespoon chopped parsley
2 teaspoons dried basil
3 tablespoons olive oil, divided
4 medium zucchini, cut into 1/4-inch-thick slices
2 green bell peppers, sliced
10 medium uncooked potatoes, skins on, chopped
4 tomatoes
1/2 cup grated Parmesan cheese

Crush the bread cubes or croutons and combine with the cottage cheese, tofu, parsley, and basil. Set aside.

Pour 2 tablespoons of the oil into a 13- by 9-inch baking dish. Arrange half of the zucchini slices, pepper slices, and chopped potatoes in the dish. Cover the layer with the reserved cottage cheese mixture. Arrange the remaining vegetables over the top in reverse order, ending with the zucchini. Drizzle with the remaining 1 tablespoon oil. Cut the tomatoes into quarters and squeeze them gently to produce some juice; then cut them into small pieces and sprinkle over the zucchini.

Cover the dish with aluminum foil and bake at 350 degrees F for 1 hour. Uncover, sprinkle the cheese over the top, and bake until nicely browned (45 minutes). Serve at once.

Serves 8.

Mexican Beans and Rice

This casserole will satisfy the heartiest of appetites. It is good accompanied by steamed cauliflower florets, on a bed of greens, garnished with sliced green onion and small slices of avocado. Serve it with very cold beer.

1 cup (7 ounces) black beans, washed and picked over
1 cup uncooked long-grain brown rice
1 cup Vegetable Stock (page 147) or water, or more as needed
2 tablespoons canola oil
1 large onion, chopped
3 large cloves garlic, minced
1 jalapeño or serrano chile, minced
2 tablespoons ground coriander
1 teaspoon salt
1/2 teaspoon freshly ground black pepper
1/4 cup shredded reduced-fat Monterey jack cheese
2 cups nonfat cottage cheese
2 medium tomatoes, sliced
4 corn tortillas, dried and broken into chips

Cover the beans with boiling water and let stand for several hours. Drain and rinse. Transfer them to a large covered pot with the rice and the stock and cook for 2 hours, adding more liquid as the mixture cooks.

In a small skillet over medium heat, warm the oil. Sauté the onion, garlic, chile, coriander, salt, and ground pepper until the vegetables are tender. Add the cheeses and stir to combine.

In a 3-quart casserole, make a layer with a third of the beans and rice mixture and half of the vegetables and cheeses. Repeat the layers, ending with beans and rice. Arrange the tomato slices over the top and bake, uncovered, at 350 degrees F until bubbly (about 30 minutes). Serve with tortilla chips.

Serves 6.

Stuffed Shells Florentine

This popular Italian dish can be made with a meat sauce, if desired. This is the vegetarian version. Italian bread and a mixed green salad go well with this meal.

1 package (12 ounces) jumbo shells
4 cups Tomato Sauce (page 147)
1 package (10 ounces) fresh spinach, stems removed, leaves chopped
1 container (15 ounces) reduced-fat ricotta cheese
8 ounces low-fat cottage cheese
8 ounces farmer cheese
2 cups shredded part-skim mozzarella cheese
2 eggs, beaten, *or* 1/2 cup egg substitute
1/4 grated Parmesan cheese

Cook the shells according to directions on page 46, omitting the oil. Rinse, drain, and set aside.

In a saucepan over medium heat, warm the Tomato Sauce. Spoon 1 cup of the sauce into the bottom of a 13- by 9-inch baking dish. Keep the remaining sauce warm.

Mix the spinach with the cheeses and eggs. With a teaspoon fill the reserved shells with the cheese mixture. Arrange the shells in a single layer on the sauce in the baking dish. Bake at 350 degrees F for 15 to 20 minutes. Pour the reserved warm sauce over the top, sprinkle with the Parmesan, and serve.

Serves 6.

Variation

Seafood Stuffed Shells. Use 4 ounces farmer cheese, 4 ounces cottage cheese, and 1 cup shredded mozzarella. To the cheese mixture add 1/2 pound cooked fresh or canned crab, flaked, and 1/2 pound small cooked shrimp. Bake as above.

Eggplant Lasagne

This modern lasagne uses tofu instead of the traditional Italian soft cheeses. It makes a trim meal indeed. Serve it with a green salad.

8 ounces lasagne noodles, preferably whole wheat or spinach
1 cup Tomato Sauce (page 147)
1 teaspoon Italian Herb Blend (page 150)
2 tablespoons all-purpose flour
1/4 teaspoon Herb and Pepper Mix (page 151)
1 medium eggplant, peeled and cut into 1/4-inch slices
1 tablespoon olive oil
1 pound soft tofu, crumbled
2 tablespoons Romano cheese

Cook the lasagne according to directions on page 46. Set aside. Heat the Tomato Sauce and stir in the herb blend. Keep warm.

Pour the flour and pepper mix into a bag and shake the eggplant slices, one at a time, to coat. Brush the eggplant lightly with the oil and arrange on a baking sheet; place under the broiler until browned (about 4 minutes on each side).

Cover the bottom of a 9-inch-square baking dish with the reserved warm sauce. Add a layer of cooked lasagne noodles, cutting to fit, and a layer of eggplant; then top with a layer of crumbled tofu and cover with more sauce. Repeat the layers, ending with lasagne. Cover with the remaining sauce. Sprinkle the cheese over the top. Cover and bake at 375 degrees F until set (about 45 minutes). Let stand for 10 minutes before serving.

Serves 6.

Variation

Mushroom and Eggplant Lasagne. Add 1/2 pound fresh mushrooms, sliced and lightly steamed, to the eggplant layer and 2 tablespoons red wine to the Tomato Sauce. Bake as above.

Cracked Wheat and Fresh Vegetables

This easy dish is a favorite in my house and is guaranteed to please a crowd of vegetarians. You can use any vegetables you have on hand. If you decide on fresh green beans, broccoli, cauliflower, or carrots, you may want to steam them a few minutes before adding them to the mixture. You can make this dish a day ahead. Crusty rye rolls or Skinny Corn Bread (page 152) make a fine accompaniment, as does chilled beer or hearty red burgundy wine.

1 cup bulgur
1 cup Vegetable Stock (page 147), boiling
3 tablespoons chopped parsley
1/4 cup diced green bell pepper
1/4 cup diced red bell pepper
1/2 cup thickly sliced green onion, including some
tops
1 cup quartered and sliced zucchini
1 cup fresh corn kernels, cut from the cob
1 cup thinly sliced carrot
2 cups reduced-fat sharp Cheddar or Monterey
jack cheese, divided
1 cup Tomato Sauce (page 147) *or* thick tomato
juice
1 tablespoon minced fresh basil *or* 1 teaspoon
crumbled dried basil
1 1/2 heaping teaspoons minced fresh oregano *or*
1/2 teaspoon crumbled dried oregano
1 large clove garlic, minced
1/2 teaspoon salt
1/4 teaspoon freshly ground white pepper
1 egg *or* 1/4 cup egg substitute

In a 13- by 9-inch baking dish, combine the bulgur and stock, mixing thoroughly. Let it stand while you prepare the vegetables.

Stir the parsley, bell peppers, green onion, zucchini, corn, and carrot into the bulgur mixture along with 1 1/2 cups of the cheese. Set aside.

Measure the Tomato Sauce, basil, oregano, garlic, salt, and ground pepper into a 4-cup measure. Beat in the egg, then stir into the bulgur mixture. Sprinkle the remaining 1/2 cup cheese over the top. (At this point you can cover the casserole and refrigerate it until the next day.)

Bake, uncovered, at 350 degrees F until the mixture is heated through and the cheese is melted (about 25 minutes, or 40 to 45 minutes if the dish has been refrigerated).

Serve hot.

Serves 4 to 6.

Variation

Cracked Wheat with Tomatoes and Zucchini. Omit the corn and carrots; increase the zucchini to 2 cups and add 1 cup cubed tomato. Substitute shredded part-skim mozzarella cheese for the Cheddar.

Vegetable Nut Roast

This is a California dish, combining all the good fresh vegetables from that region. Serve it with warm Tomato Sauce (page 147) or, if you like a Mexican influence, Dick's Salsa (page 149) or Green Chile Salsa (page 149). A salad of romaine and orange sections with Creamy Orange Dressing (page 150) makes a good accompaniment.

2 tablespoons vegetable oil
1 large onion, chopped
1 1/2 cups chopped fresh mushrooms
2 cloves garlic, minced
1 green bell pepper, chopped
1 teaspoon dried thyme
1 teaspoon dried winter savory
1/2 teaspoon rubbed dried sage
1/2 teaspoon freshly ground white pepper
1 1/2 cups cooked brown rice
1 cup walnuts, finely chopped
1/2 cup cashews, finely chopped
2 eggs, beaten, *or* 1/2 cup egg substitute
1 1/2 cups nonfat cottage cheese
1 1/2 cups mixed shredded cheeses, such as reduced-fat Cheddar, Monterey jack, Sap Sago,
   Parmesan, or fontina
1/4 cup minced parsley
Vegetable spray, for loaf pan
Carrot and celery sticks, for garnish
Tomato slices, for garnish

In a large skillet over medium heat, warm the oil. Sauté the onion until it begins to soften. Add the mushrooms, garlic, bell pepper, thyme, savory, sage, and ground pepper. Cook until the bell pepper is soft. Mix in the rice, nuts, eggs, cottage cheese, shredded cheeses, and parsley; blend well. Taste for seasoning, noting that the saltiness of the cheeses will be brought out by cooking.

Spray a 9- by 5-inch loaf pan with vegetable spray. Spoon the loaf mixture into the pan and smooth out the top. Bake at 350 degrees F until firm (about 1 hour).

Let the pan cool on a wire rack for about 10 minutes. Invert the loaf onto a serving platter, garnish with the carrot and celery sticks and tomato slices, and serve.

Serves 6.

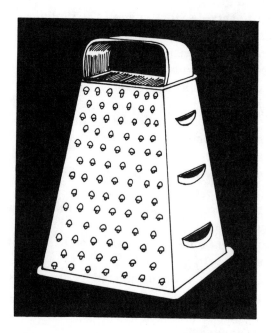

Pizza Riso

This variation of a popular Italian dish has a savory crust of seasoned rice. It's quick to make and an interesting change. Serve it with tender green beans, a mixed green salad, and good Italian red wine.

1 cup coarsely grated carrot
2 1/2 cups cooked brown rice
1/3 cup whole wheat pastry flour
1/2 cup low-fat cottage cheese
2 tablespoons minced onion
1 teaspoon Italian Herb Blend (page 150)
Vegetable spray, for baking pan
3/4 cup Tomato Sauce (page 147)
2 small zucchini, sliced
1 green bell pepper, sliced
1 cup sliced fresh mushrooms
1 cup shredded part-skim mozzarella cheese

Place the carrot in a strainer and cover with a weighted bowl. Let drain for about 15 minutes, then pat dry. Combine the drained carrot with the rice, flour, cottage cheese, onion, and 1/2 teaspoon of the herb blend.

Coat a 13- by 9-inch baking pan with vegetable spray. Spread the carrot mixture on the bottom of the pan and 1/4 inch up the sides. (For a round pizza, spread the carrot mixture on a pizza pan and pinch up the edges to form a low rim.) Bake at 350 degrees F for 25 minutes. Put it under the broiler for a few minutes to brown the crust; watch carefully, since the carrot can burn very quickly.

Spread the Tomato Sauce over the hot crust, arrange the zucchini, bell pepper, and mushrooms over the sauce, and top with the cheese. Sprinkle the remaining 1/2 teaspoon of the herb blend over the cheese and bake until the vegetables are tender and the cheese is browned and bubbly (20 to 25 minutes). Serve hot.

Serves 8.

Onion and Basil Pie

Here is a tasty pie with no pie crust and lots of flavor from the herbs. It is easily made with a food processor. Serve it with a shredded spinach salad with sliced tomatoes and Creamy Vinaigrette (page 149).

2 tablespoons olive oil, divided
2 cups thinly sliced onion
3 cups low-fat cottage cheese or farmer cheese
1/4 cup toasted pine nuts
3 large cloves garlic
2 tablespoons minced parsley, preferably flat-
   leaf (Italian)
1/2 cup fresh basil leaves
2 tablespoons lemon juice
2 eggs, beaten, *or* 1/2 cup egg substitute
1/4 cup grated Sap Sago or Romano cheese
1/4 teaspoon freshly grated nutmeg
1/4 teaspoon freshly ground black pepper
Vegetable spray, for pan

In a large nonstick skillet over medium heat, warm 1 tablespoon of the oil. Sauté the onion until soft (about 8 minutes). Let it cool.

In a food processor blend the cottage cheese, pine nuts, garlic, parsley, and basil, pulsing on and off until well combined. With the motor running, gradually add the lemon juice and the remaining 1 tablespoon oil. Mix until thick.

Stir the cottage cheese mixture into the sautéed onion along with the eggs, cheese, nutmeg, and ground pepper. Mix well. Pour the mixture into a 9-inch springform pan coated with vegetable spray. Bake at 350 degrees F until a knife inserted in the center comes out clean (50 to 60 minutes). Let it cool on a wire rack for about 20 minutes. Remove the outside of the pan and cut the pie into wedges to serve.

Serves 6.

Stuffed Acorn Squash

Yellow vegetables are getting good press these days because they contain beta-carotene, believed to be an excellent cancer-prevention agent. Health benefits aside, winter squashes are simply delicious and provide superb receptacles for vegetable stuffings. Because the stuffing in this dish is slightly sweet, serve it with tender fresh whole green beans, garnished with fresh dill and a squeeze of lemon juice.

Skinny Corn Bread (page 152), at room temperature
Vegetable spray, for baking dish
2 large acorn squash, halved lengthwise, seeds discarded
2 tablespoons olive oil
1/4 cup diced onion
1/4 cup diced celery
1/4 cup sunflower seeds
1/4 cup raisins
1/2 teaspoon dried sage
1/2 teaspoon freshly grated nutmeg
1/4 teaspoon freshly ground white pepper
1/2 cup apple cider or unsweetened apple juice, or more as needed

Crumble the corn bread (it can be baked the day, or days, before) into a large bowl and set aside.

Coat a 13- by 9-inch baking dish with vegetable spray. Arrange the squash, cut side down, in the dish and pour in a small amount of water. Bake at 350 degrees F until the squash is barely tender (45 minutes). Let cool slightly, then scoop out flesh, leaving a 1/2-inch-thick shell. Set the shells aside. Mash the flesh slightly and add to the reserved corn bread.

In a small skillet over medium heat, warm the oil. Sauté the onion, celery, and sunflower seeds until the onion is tender. Stir in the raisins, sage, nutmeg, ground pepper, and apple juice. Mix well, then pour over the corn bread mixture and toss lightly to mix. If necessary, add a little more juice to make a moist mixture.

Mound the stuffing into the reserved shells. If you have too much stuffing to fit, bake the extra in a small bowl and serve it on the side. Bake at 350 degrees F until heated through (about 20 minutes). Serve hot.

Serves 4.

Stove-top Dishes

We generally think of stove-top cooking as a quick kind of meal preparation, even though stews and some curries take considerable cooking time. The basic stir-fry, for example, means having the various ingredients prepared in advance, with the actual cooking being done in a hurry; such cooking requires concentration for a short time and I always enjoy watching someone else do it. The recipes here generally offer a more relaxed approach to cooking, and many of them involve a long, slow process.

This chapter is divided into two sections: the first, on skillet dishes, includes stir-fry meals, grain dishes, pasta sauces, and most curries; the second section is on stews—the dishes that generally need a longer time simmering on the back of the stove.

Skillet Dishes

The best-known and most popular skillet dishes come from the rich Asian traditions and are as varied as the cultures from that part of the world. The basic stir-fry is quick, uses fresh foods, and probably represents the most adaptability in cooking methods and use of ingredients. Stir-frying can be used with leftover foods as well as fresh, and the combinations are almost limitless.

If you have a wok, this is the time to use it. Just heat the oil until it is quite hot and then stir-fry the various ingredients, pushing them up the side of the wok as they finish cooking. Watching a good Asian cook who has mastered this technique is a true pleasure. The stir-fry is then served over hot rice— short-grain and slightly sticky in the true Asian tradition—or Asian noodles.

Also included in the skillet dishes are popular grain dishes, including pilaf and risotto. Much has been written recently about true risotto. An explanation is given on page 70. The process involves standing over the stove for most of a half hour,

adding stock to the rice at intervals and stirring a lot. The end result is creamy and truly Italian. A simpler stove-top meal, however, is grain pilaf, in which the grains are browned in oil with vegetables; then the liquid is added all at once and the dish cooks, undisturbed, until the grains are done, usually within half an hour.

The toppings for pasta, like the stir-fries, offer almost unlimited combinations of ingredients, a good place to use your imagination.

Remember that the skillet dishes represent probably the quickest cooking meals you will find in this book. They are particularly valuable because of the large amounts of complex carbohydrates found in the whole grains and pastas used.

Note on cooking pasta: Because much of the pasta recommended in these recipes does not come in a package necessarily, here are general indications for cooking it. Use a large pot. Heat the water (4 quarts per 1 pound pasta) to a rolling boil. Add 1/4 teaspoon salt for each 2 quarts water and a small amount of olive or canola oil. Add the pasta to the boiling water and stir vigorously with a wooden spoon to separate it. Reduce the heat to medium-low and cook, boiling, until the pasta reaches what the Italians call al dente, that is, cooked but firm and slightly resistant to the bite. Lift out a piece or strand to test it. This takes between 5 and 10 minutes depending on the type of pasta used. Pour immediately into a colander and shake well to get rid of the water. If using with a sauce, serve at once.

Beef with Broccoli and Red Peppers

This Asian-style dish is easily and quickly made. Serve it over hot short-grain brown or white rice. Begin the meal with a quick Chinese vegetable soup, made by heating 4 cups water, 1 can sliced mushrooms, 1 can sliced water chestnuts, 1/4 cup sliced bamboo shoots, 2 sliced green onions, 1 tablespoon low-sodium soy sauce, and 1 tablespoon dry sherry. Chilled beer is a good accompaniment.

1 tablespoon vegetable oil
12 ounces top round steak, cut into thin strips
4 cups small broccoli pieces (stems and florets)
1 large red bell pepper, cut into strips
1 large clove garlic, sliced thin
1/4 cup low-sodium soy sauce
1 tablespoon cornstarch
1/4 teaspoon freshly ground white pepper
1/2 cup Beef Stock (page 146)
1 cup water
1 cup sliced green onion, with tops
3 to 4 cups hot cooked rice

In a large skillet over medium heat, warm the oil. Add the meat and brown slightly. Stir in the broccoli, bell pepper, garlic, and soy sauce. Cover the pan and let simmer until the vegetables are barely tender (about 8 minutes).

Blend the cornstarch and ground pepper into the stock. Add to the meat mixture along with the water and green onion. Cook, stirring constantly, until the sauce is thickened. Serve immediately over the hot rice.

Serves 6 to 8.

Sukiyaki

Serve this easy and delicious Japanese dish with a salad of bean sprouts and cucumber and zesty Sesame Dressing (page 150).

12 ounces beef flank steak, cut 1 inch thick, frozen for 30 minutes
4 tablespoons dry white wine, divided
4 tablespoons low-sodium soy sauce, divided
1 1/2 cups Beef Stock (page 146)
1 tablespoon sugar
1 tablespoon vegetable oil
2 medium onions, sliced thin
2 medium carrots, cut into 1/2-inch diagonal slices
2 stalks celery, cut into 1/2-inch diagonal slices
1/4 pound fresh mushrooms, sliced
4 green onions, cut into 1-inch pieces
8 ounces fine rice noodles (rice sticks)
4 cups packed spinach leaves, rinsed, stemmed, and torn into bite-sized pieces

Cut the briefly frozen beef into 1/8-inch-thick slices and place in a bowl. Add 2 tablespoons of the wine and 2 tablespoons of the soy sauce; stir well. Let marinate while preparing the vegetables.

Combine the stock and sugar with the remaining 2 tablespoons wine and 2 tablespoons soy sauce. In a large skillet over medium heat, warm the oil. Sauté the onions, carrots, celery, mushrooms, and green onions. Add the stock mixture and noodles and simmer for 8 minutes. Stir in the meat and marinade and cook until the meat loses its red color. Add the spinach and cook for 2 minutes longer. Serve hot.

Serves 4.

Curried Beef and Rice

Curried dishes have long been a staple food of Southeast Asia, especially India, and some of them come very hot indeed. I shall never forget how much my throat hurt after I ate curry for the first time. If you like your curry mild, use less curry powder or a milder form of it. Serve this dish with Indian flatbread and a salad of shredded carrot and raisins with a sweet honey dressing. Do avoid two of the usual curry accompaniments, finely chopped hard-cooked egg and grated coconut, both very high in saturated fat.

1 cup uncooked long-grain brown rice
12 ounces lean top round steak, all visible fat
 removed
1 tablespoon curry powder
1/4 teaspoon salt
Generous dash cayenne pepper
1 teaspoon canola oil
1 cup coarsely chopped onion
2 cloves garlic, minced
1 cup Beef Stock (page 146)
2 cups low-sodium canned tomatoes, with juice
1/2 cup raisins
1/4 cup chopped unsalted roasted peanuts

Measure the rice into a large bowl and add enough boiling water to cover. Set aside.

Cut the steak into small cubes. Combine the curry, salt, and cayenne and mix well; reserve 1 teaspoon and sprinkle the remaining mixture evenly over the steak.

In a large skillet with a lid, warm the oil over medium-high heat. Add the steak and cook until it loses its pink color (about 4 minutes). Remove the steak from the skillet and set aside.

Add the onion and garlic to the skillet and sauté for several minutes. Drain the rice and add it to the skillet along with the reserved 1 teaspoon curry mixture, stock, and tomatoes. Cover and bring to a boil, then reduce the heat and simmer until the liquid is absorbed (about 30 minutes).

Add the raisins and reserved steak and stir well. Turn off the heat and let stand, covered, for 5 minutes. Top with the peanuts and serve.

Serves 6.

Variation

Curried Lamb and Rice. Instead of beef, substitute 12 ounces boneless lamb (all visible fat removed), cut into 3/4-inch cubes. If desired, stir in 1/2 cup plain low-fat yogurt with the raisins and meat and heat through.

Macaroni alla Napoletana

This Italian dish has been a family favorite for years. It is very quick and nourishing. If possible, use fresh beans (broad flat Italian beans are the best) and flat-leaf (Italian) parsley. The dish is delicious with garlic bread and light Italian red wine.

1/2 pound lean ground beef
2 ounces mild Italian turkey sausage or Italian sweet sausage, skin removed, cut into small pieces
8 ounces elbow macaroni, small shells, or spirals
1/2 cup chopped onion
1 large clove garlic, minced
1 1/2 cups low-sodium canned tomatoes, with juice
1 cup cut green beans, fresh or frozen
1 tablespoon chopped parsley
1 teaspoon Italian Herb Blend (page 150)
1/2 teaspoon salt (less if the tomatoes contain salt)
1/2 teaspoon freshly ground black pepper, or more as needed
1 1/2 cups Vegetable Stock (page 147) or water
4 ounces part-skim mozzarella cheese, diced very small

In a large skillet with a lid, brown the ground beef and sausage over medium heat, stirring to break up the meat. Remove the meat from the pan, spread on paper towels, and blot most of the fat with paper towels. Add the macaroni, onion, and garlic to the pan and brown them until golden. Then return the meat to the pan and add the tomatoes, beans, parsley, herb blend, salt, ground pepper, and stock. Cover and simmer for 30 minutes.

Taste and add more ground pepper if desired. Stir in the mozzarella and serve immediately.

Serves 4.

Pilaf, Greek Style

Unlike the usual pilaf, the rice in this one is already cooked, and the dish contains beef. Serve this with a classic Greek salad of greens, black olives, and feta cheese with a simple lemon and olive oil dressing. Accompany it with hearty red wine.

3/4 pound lean ground beef
1 cup chopped onion
1 large clove garlic, minced
1 cup sliced celery
1 1/2 cups thinly sliced zucchini
2 cups chopped tomato
2 teaspoons dried oregano
1 teaspoon dried dill weed
1/2 teaspoon salt
1/2 teaspoon freshly ground black pepper
1 package (10 ounces) frozen chopped spinach
3 cups cooked brown rice
1/2 cup quick-cooking rolled oats
Vegetable Stock (page 147) or tomato juice, as needed
2 tablespoons grated Sap Sago or Romano cheese
Lemon wedges, for garnish

In a large skillet or flameproof casserole with a lid, brown the beef with the onion and garlic over medium heat. Stir in the celery, zucchini, tomato, oregano, dill, salt, ground pepper, and frozen spinach. Cover and simmer until the spinach is defrosted and the vegetables are tender.

Add the cooked rice and rolled oats; cover and cook for about 5 minutes. If the dish seems too dry, add vegetable stock or tomato juice.

Serve with the cheese sprinkled over the top and with the lemon wedges, which should be squeezed over the dish to add a lemon-juice garnish.

Serves 6 generously.

Swedish Meatballs
and Pilaf

Meatballs have always been a popular and tasty way to extend the meat in a recipe. They often are added to a tomato sauce for pasta. This meatball dish with vegetables and a slightly creamy sauce has many ingredients but is quickly and easily made. Good accompaniments would be hearty rye bread and cole slaw with diced apple, orange sections, and seedless grapes and topped with Orange Ginger Dressing (page 150).

3/4 pound lean ground beef
1/2 cup wheat germ
1/4 cup dry whole wheat bread crumbs
3/4 cup skim milk
1/4 cup finely chopped onion
1/4 cup egg substitute *or* 1 egg, beaten
1 tablespoon Worcestershire sauce
1/4 teaspoon salt
1/4 teaspoon freshly ground black pepper
1 large onion, sliced thin and separated into rings
1 cup Beef Stock (page 146), or more as needed
1/2 pound sliced fresh mushrooms
2 cups frozen or fresh peas
1 1/2 cups cooked brown rice

Caper Sauce

l tablespoon all-purpose flour
1/2 cup skim milk
1/2 cup plain low-fat yogurt
2 tablespoons drained capers
1/4 teaspoon salt

In a large bowl prepare the meatballs: Combine the ground beef, wheat germ, bread crumbs, skim milk, chopped onion, egg substitute, Worcestershire sauce, salt, and ground pepper; mix well.

Shape the mixture into 18 balls. Place them in the center of a large skillet or flameproof casserole with a lid. Distribute the onion rings around them and cook over medium heat until the meatballs are brown and the onions are golden. Reduce the heat and add the stock. Deglaze the pan by scraping up the browned bits from the bottom and stirring. Add the mushrooms and peas, cover, and simmer for about 15 minutes.

While the meatballs are cooking, prepare the sauce: In a small saucepan over medium heat, combine the flour and milk and cook, stirring constantly, until thickened. Reduce the heat and stir in the yogurt, capers, and salt. Keep warm but do not boil.

Add the rice to the meatballs and vegetables and cook just long enough to heat the rice thoroughly. Pour the sauce over top and stir well. Add more stock if the mixture is too dry. Serve hot.

Serves 6.

Variations

Meatballs with Bulgur. Substitute 1 1/2 cups cooked bulgur for the brown rice.

Texas Meatball Stew with Rice. Substitute 1 1/2 teaspoons chili powder for the Worcestershire sauce. Instead of mushrooms and peas, use 1 can (16 ounces) tomatoes with juice, 2 cups fresh or frozen corn kernels, and 1 large green bell pepper. Omit the Caper Sauce and serve right from the stew pot with Skinny Corn Bread (page 152).

Veal Shanks à la Grecque

Veal is an expensive meat, but the shanks are reasonably priced and rich in protein. Cut away any visible fat and enjoy these unusual flavors. Serve this with Simple Garlic Bread (page 152) and a spinach and mixed green salad with lemon and olive oil dressing.

All-purpose flour, for dredging
1/4 teaspoon salt
1/4 teaspoon freshly ground white pepper
2 tablespoons olive oil
3 1/2 pounds veal shank, bone in, cut crosswise
    into 2-inch pieces
1 cup finely chopped onion
1 cup finely chopped celery
1 large clove garlic, minced
2 1/4 cups Chicken Stock (page 146)
1 cup chopped tomato, fresh or canned
1 cup thinly sliced zucchini
1 cup thinly sliced summer squash
1/2 cup dry white wine
2 tablespoons finely chopped fresh dill weed *or* 2
    teaspoons dried dill weed
1 bay leaf
1/4 cup orzo *or* short-grain white rice

Season the flour with the salt and ground pepper, and dredge the veal in it. In a large heavy skillet with a lid, warm the oil over medium heat. Brown the veal, turning often. Pour the fat from the skillet, then scatter the onion, celery, and garlic around the meat. Cook, stirring, until the vegetables are soft.

Add 1/2 cup of the stock and stir to scrape up the browned bits on the bottom and sides of the skillet. Add the tomato, zucchini, squash, wine, dill, and bay leaf. Cover closely and simmer for 30 minutes. Then add the remaining 1 3/4 cups stock and the orzo stirring well. Cover closely and cook for 15 minutes longer. Discard the bay leaf before serving.

Serves 6.

Pork with Yams, Bok Choy, and Rice

This Asian dish contains some especially healthful ingredients. Begin the meal with a light chicken and watercress soup.

1 tablespoon sesame oil
1/2 pound lean pork tenderloin, all visible fat
    removed, sliced into very thin strips
4 green onions, sliced
1/2 pound bok choy or Chinese cabbage, cut into
    1-inch pieces (2 1/2 cups)
1 medium clove garlic, minced
2 thin slices fresh ginger, peeled and minced
3/4 cup short-grain white rice
2 cups water
2 medium yams, peeled and cut into 3/4-inch
    cubes (6 cups)
3 tablespoons dry sherry
2 tablespoons hoisin sauce

In a large skillet over medium-high heat, warm the oil. Add the pork and stir-fry until it is lightly browned (about 5 minutes). Increase the heat to high; add the green onions, bok choy, garlic, and fresh ginger. Cook, stirring, for 2 minutes.

Stir in the rice and the water and bring to a boil. Mix in the yams, sherry, and hoisin sauce and return to a boil, then reduce the heat to low, cover, and simmer until the yams and rice are cooked (30 to 35 minutes). Serve hot.

Serves 4 to 6.

Pork Chops Braised in Beer with Red Cabbage

Here is a leaner and quicker-cooking version of a traditional German dinner. It makes a hearty winter meal served with thick slices of dark rye bread and chilled beer.

4 center-cut pork chops, bone in, each 1 1/4-inches thick (about 2 pounds total), all visible fat removed
1/2 teaspoon salt, or more as needed
1/2 teaspoon freshly ground black pepper, or more as needed
1 tablespoon canola oil
1 large red onion, sliced thin
1 tablespoon Dijon mustard
1 small head red cabbage, cored and sliced thin
1 large Granny Smith apple, sliced thin lengthwise
2 large potatoes, sliced thin
1 cup beer
1 1/2 teaspoons caraway seeds
1/2 teaspoon dried summer savory
1/4 cup Chicken Stock (page 146)

Sprinkle the pork chops with the salt and ground pepper. In a large skillet with a lid, warm the oil over medium heat. Brown the chops on both sides (about 8 minutes in all). Remove the chops, cover, and keep warm.

Add the onion to the skillet and sauté until soft (about 2 minutes). Add the mustard, cabbage, and apple; sauté until the cabbage is lightly browned (about 2 minutes).

Add potatoes, beer, and caraway seeds, bring to a boil, and simmer until the cabbage wilts (about 4 minutes).

Return the pork chops to the skillet, covering them with the cabbage mixture. Add the savory and stock. Cover and simmer until the chops are cooked through and the potatoes are done (about 20 minutes). Season with more salt and ground pepper, if desired. Serve immediately.

Serves 4 generously.

Thai Pork with Cellophane Noodles

Cellophane noodles (also called Chinese vermicelli) are made from mung beans and are transparent before they are cooked. You can find them, and the fermented black beans called for here, in Asian markets.

3/4 cup cellophane noodles
5 tablespoons Vegetable Stock (page 147)
2 tablespoons fermented black beans, rinsed and chopped
1 tablespoon sweet rice vinegar
2 teaspoons cornstarch
1 large clove garlic, minced
1 thin slice fresh ginger, peeled and minced
1/2 pound lean pork tenderloin, all visible fat removed, sliced very thin
1 cup shredded fresh spinach
1/2 cup slivered red bell pepper
1/2 cup chopped water chestnuts

In a large mixing bowl, cover the noodles with boiling water and let soak for 20 minutes. Drain and cut into 1-inch pieces with scissors. Set aside.

In a small bowl combine 2 tablespoons of the stock with the beans, vinegar, and cornstarch. Set aside.

In a wok or sauté pan over medium heat, warm the remaining 3 tablespoons stock. Add the garlic and ginger and cook for 2 minutes. Stir in the pork and reserved noodles and simmer until the pork is cooked through (about 3 minutes). Add the spinach, bell pepper, water chestnuts, and reserved bean mixture. Cook until the sauce is clear, tossing to heat all the ingredients. Serve immediately.

Serves 4.

Cannellini e Pepperoni

This combination of legumes, greens, and pasta represents Italian country cooking at its best. Use pepperoni made from turkey, if at all possible. Serve this with beer or red wine and crusty whole-grain country bread. Note that the dried beans must be soaked overnight before using.

1 pound dried cannellini beans *or* 2 cans (19 ounces each) cannellini, rinsed and drained
3 pounds Swiss chard or collard greens
1 tablespoon olive oil
5 cloves garlic, chopped fine
1/4 pound pepperoni, sliced thin and cut in half
2 tablespoons chopped flat-leaf (Italian) parsley
1 tablespoon chopped fresh oregano *or* 1 teaspoon dried oregano
1 cup uncooked vegetable spiral pasta or elbow macaroni
3/4 cup Vegetable Stock (page 147)
1 1/2 cups water
Salt and freshly ground pepper, to taste

If using dried beans, pour boiling water over them and soak overnight; drain thoroughly.

Trim the Swiss chard and blanch in boiling water for 2 minutes. Drain and chop coarsely.

In a heavy pot with a lid, warm the oil over medium heat. Sauté the garlic until golden. Add the pepperoni, parsley, and oregano and sauté for 1 minute. Add the pasta, stock, water, reserved chard, and reserved beans (see Note). Taste and adjust the seasoning (the amount of salt needed depends a great deal on the pepperoni used).

Cover and cook over low heat for 45 to 50 minutes, stirring occasionally. Serve hot.

Serves 6 to 8.

Note: If using canned beans, add them to the pot 10 minutes before the end of the cooking time.

Chicken with Cashews

This Chinese dish, called *U Quo Chow Gai Ding*, provides the opportunity to do an authentic stir-fry. Although there are several separate receptacles involved, everything eventually is combined and cooked in one pan. The secret is to assemble all the ingredients before you start to cook. Serve this dish with lots of hot short-grain rice, preferably brown, and hot tea.

2 tablespoons cornstarch
1 tablespoon dry sherry
1 teaspoon low-sodium soy sauce
1-inch piece fresh ginger, peeled and minced
1 medium chicken breast quarter (about 8 ounces), skinned, boned, and cut into 1/2-inch cubes
1/4 pound fresh mushrooms, sliced
Half a 5-ounce can water chestnuts, drained and sliced
Half an 8-ounce can sliced bamboo shoots, drained and cut into 1/2-inch cubes
1 cup (about 3 ounces) snow peas cut in half, ends trimmed
3/4 cup Chicken Stock (page 146)
1 tablespoon peanut oil
1/4 cup whole raw cashews
1/4 teaspoon salt
1 large clove garlic, minced
1 large onion, halved, then sliced
4 cups hot cooked short-grain brown rice (see Appendix for cooking indications)

In a medium bowl combine 1 tablespoon of the cornstarch, the sherry, soy sauce, and fresh ginger. Stir in the chicken and set aside to marinate for at least 15 minutes.

In a large bowl combine the mushrooms, water chestnuts, bamboo shoots, and snow peas; set aside. In a 1-cup measure mix together the stock and the remaining 1 tablespoon cornstarch; set aside.

In a wok or sauté pan over medium heat, warm the oil until hot. Add the nuts and stir-fry until lightly browned. (Watch carefully; this happens quickly.) Remove the nuts with a slotted spoon and set aside. Add the salt, garlic, and onion and stir-fry until they are golden.

Add the reserved chicken mixture and stir until the chicken starts to brown (about 3 minutes). Add the reserved vegetables and stir for 2 minutes. Add the reserved stock mixture and stir until it comes to a boil and thickens. Turn off the heat, cover the pan, and let the mixture stand for 2 to 3 minutes. Stir in the reserved cashews and serve immediately on the hot rice.

Serves 4.

Herbed Chicken and Rice, Venetian Style

The popular combination of rice and peas called *risi e bisi* is eaten all over Western Europe. In northern Italy the dish is more like a soup. The adaptation here uses less liquid and adds chicken to make a complete meal (see Note). You could accompany it with a *macedonia* (a combination of mixed fresh fruits) and crisp white wine.

1 tablespoon light margarine
3 green onions, chopped fine
1 cup short-grain white rice
1/2 teaspoon dried crushed basil *or* 1 1/2 teaspoons minced fresh basil
1/2 teaspoon dried lemon thyme *or* 1 teaspoon minced fresh lemon thyme
2 1/2 cups Chicken Stock (page 146), heated
2 chicken breast quarters (about 12 ounces each), skin and all visible fat removed
2 cups frozen tiny peas
1/4 cup grated Parmesan cheese

In a heavy skillet or pot with a lid, melt the margarine over medium heat. Sauté the green onions and rice, stirring, until the rice is golden. Gently stir in the basil, thyme, and stock. Reduce the heat, cover, and simmer for 15 minutes.

With a sharp knife cut the chicken meat from the bone and into strips (about 2 inches long and 1/4 inch wide). Add it to the pot, stir well, cover, and cook until the chicken is steamed through and tender (about 10 minutes).

Stir in the peas (it is not necessary to defrost them) and cook just enough to heat them thoroughly (no more than 2 minutes). Remove the pot from the heat, sprinkle the cheese over all, toss lightly to fluff the rice, and serve immediately.

Serves 6.

Note: This dish can also be made as a true risotto, by adding the stock in three parts and stirring frequently. For this method, see page 70.

Variations

Herbed Pork with Rice. Use pork instead of chicken: Sauté 1 cup pork in strips (either fresh from the loin or leftover from a roast, all visible fat removed) in the margarine before adding the green onions and rice. Substitute 1 teaspoon summer savory for the basil. Proceed as above.

Wehani Rice with Chicken. Omit the herbs and Parmesan cheese. Sauté 1 small carrot, sliced, with the onions and substitute 2 cups Wehani rice for the white rice. When adding the chicken, stir in 1/4 cup port wine, 1/4 teaspoon each salt and freshly ground white pepper, and 2 tablespoons minced parsley. Garnish with 1/3 cup chopped pecans, toasted.

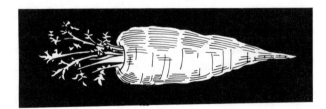

Linguini with Chicken and Zucchini

This is one of the simplest pasta sauces ever. If you have any leftover cooked chicken, your meal can be ready in just a few minutes. Serve it with Simple Garlic Bread (page 152) and a salad of mixed greens and tomato wedges.

1 tablespoon olive oil
1 medium onion, chopped
1 large clove garlic, minced
1/4 pound fresh mushrooms, sliced
1/2 cup water
1 cup finely chopped cooked chicken
1 teaspoon rubbed dried sage
1/2 teaspoon salt
1/2 teaspoon freshly ground white pepper
1/2 cup dry white wine
2 cups cubed zucchini (1/4-inch pieces)
8 ounces linguini, flat spinach pasta, or whole
  wheat spirals
3 quarts water
4 tablespoons Romano or Sap Sago cheese

In a heavy skillet with a lid, warm the oil over medium heat. Add the onion, garlic, and mushrooms and sauté until the onions are transparent. Stir in the water, chicken, sage, salt, wine, and zucchini. Cover and steam for 10 minutes.

Meanwhile, boil the pasta in the water until al dente (about 7 minutes). Drain and place on 4 warm serving plates or bowls. Spoon the chicken mixture over the pasta. Sprinkle the cheese over all. Serve at once.

Serves 4.

Variation

Linguini with Chicken and Fresh Tomatoes. Instead of zucchini, use 10 ounces fresh spinach, washed, stems removed, torn into pieces, and 2 large tomatoes, cut into pieces. Reduce the water to 1/4 cup and substitute 1 teaspoon dried basil for the sage.

Turkey Stroganoff

Traditionally this dish is made with thin strips of beef and sour cream. This updated version uses leaner ingredients—turkey and low-fat yogurt. Accompany it with a salad of thinly sliced cucumbers, chilled in a yogurt sauce (1 clove garlic, crushed and mixed with 2 cups plain low-fat yogurt and 1/4 teaspoon chopped dried mint), and dark Russian rye bread.

1 tablespoon canola oil
1 medium onion, chopped
1/2 pound fresh mushrooms, sliced
1 tablespoon all-purpose flour
2 teaspoons paprika
1/2 teaspoon salt
1/2 teaspoon dried basil
1/4 teaspoon dried thyme
1/2 cup Chicken Stock (page 146)
1/2 cup dry white wine
1/2 cup plain low-fat yogurt
2 cups diced cooked turkey breast
2 teaspoons lemon juice
2 tablespoons chopped fresh dill weed *or* 2 teaspoons dried dill weed
6 ounces light egg noodles, cooked, drained, and
  kept hot

In a large saucepan or Dutch oven over medium heat, warm the oil. Add the onion and sauté until golden. Add the mushrooms and cook, stirring, for 3 to 5 minutes.

Blend in the flour, paprika, salt, basil, and thyme. Gradually stir in the stock and wine. Cook, stirring constantly, until the mixture thickens and bubbles for a minute; then cover and simmer for 5 minutes. Remove from the heat.

Blend in the yogurt. Add the turkey, lemon juice, and dill. Heat thoroughly over low heat but do not boil. Serve over the hot noodles.

Serves 4.

Variation

Veal Stroganoff. Instead of turkey, use 1 pound boneless veal, all visible fat removed, cut into thin strips. Sauté it with the onion so that it cooks in the sauce. Serve as above.

Turkey Curry

This dish is my favorite way of using turkey left over from the holidays. It is invariably delicious, and very quickly made. You can serve the usual curry accompaniments—grated coconut (but use only sparingly, please, since it is high in saturated fat) and chopped unsalted roasted peanuts. Start cooking the rice accompaniment about 40 minutes before you start making the curry so that everything will be done at the same time.

1 tablespoon light margarine
1 large onion, chopped fine
1 cup thinly sliced celery
1 tart apple, chopped
1/2 teaspoon minced peeled fresh ginger *or* 1/2
   teaspoon ground ginger
2 tablespoons all-purpose flour
1 tablespoon curry powder
1/8 teaspoon ground cumin
2 cups Turkey Stock (page 146)
3 cups shredded cooked turkey
1/2 cup raisins
3 cups hot cooked long-grain brown rice

In a large stove-top casserole with a lid, melt the margarine over medium heat. Sauté the onion, celery, apple, and fresh ginger until tender but not browned. (If you use ground ginger, add it with the curry). Sprinkle the flour, curry, and cumin over the top and cook, stirring, for 2 minutes.

Stir in the stock and bring to a boil, stirring constantly. Cook until thickened. Add the turkey and heat thoroughly; do not boil. Stir in the raisins. Serve immediately over the hot rice.

Serves 6.

Turkey Ham & Pineapple, Hawaiian Style

This dish is low in fat and high in flavor. Be sure to use unsweetened pineapple, and turkey ham. Serve it with a mixed green salad topped with Slim Yogurt Dressing (page 149).

1 tablespoon light margarine
1 cup diagonally sliced carrot (1/4 inch thick)
1 cup diagonally sliced celery
3 green onions, diagonally sliced into 1-inch pieces
1 large clove garlic, minced
1 teaspoon minced peeled fresh ginger
1 can (8 ounces) pineapple chunks, drained and
   juice reserved
1 tablespoon cornstarch
1 tablespoon low-sodium soy sauce
1 teaspoon lemon juice
1 teaspoon Chinese five-spice powder
1/2 teaspoon freshly ground white pepper
2 cups diced turkey ham (1/2-inch pieces)
1 can (5 ounces) water chestnuts, drained and
   sliced thin
4 cups hot cooked short-grain brown rice (see
   Appendix for cooking indications)

In a flameproof casserole with a lid, melt the margarine over medium heat. Add the carrot, celery, green onions, garlic, and fresh ginger; sauté until the vegetables are crisp-tender. Remove from the heat and set aside.

Measure the pineapple juice into a 2-cup measure. Add enough water to make 1 1/4 cups. Blend in the cornstarch, soy sauce, lemon juice, spice powder, and ground pepper. Stir into the reserved vegetable mixture and cook, stirring, until thickened.

Add the pineapple, ham, and water chestnuts. Heat thoroughly. Serve over the hot rice.

Serves 6.

Cod, Spanish Style

This dish is traditionally made with hake, Spain's most popular fish. This adaptation uses cod, which is a member of the same family. For a complete meal, serve it with a mixed green salad and dry white wine.

1 1/2 pounds new potatoes, sliced thin
1 tablespoon olive oil
2 large cloves garlic, minced
1 large onion, sliced
4 medium carrots, sliced fine
4 tablespoons Crushed Tomatoes (page 148) or
**   tomato paste**
1 tablespoon white wine vinegar
1 cup dry white wine
1 cup water
1 bay leaf
1 teaspoon dried thyme
1/2 teaspoon salt
1/2 teaspoon cayenne pepper
4 cod steaks (each 4 to 6 ounces), about 1 inch
**   thick, rinsed and patted dry**
3 tablespoons chopped parsley

In a medium saucepan over medium-high heat, steam the potatoes in a small amount of water until tender (about 10 minutes).

Meanwhile, in a nonstick skillet with a lid, warm the oil over medium-high heat. Sauté the garlic, onion, and carrots until the onion softens. Stir in the tomatoes, vinegar, wine, water, bay leaf, thyme, salt, and cayenne. Cover, reduce the heat, and let simmer. Drain the cooked potatoes and add them to the onion mixture.

Place the fish in the skillet, under the vegetables and sauce, and cook for about 10 minutes. Discard the bay leaf, sprinkle the parsley on top, and serve.

Serves 4.

Variations

Haddock, Spanish Style. Substitute 4 haddock fillets (4 to 6 ounces each) for the cod.

Monkfish, Spanish Style. Substitute 3/4 to 1 pound monkfish for the cod. Reduce the water to 1/2 cup and add 1 red bell pepper, cut into strips, and 4 medium tomatoes, peeled and chopped.

Tuna Spaghetti with Yogurt

This quick and easy pasta dish is a rather unusual combination of tuna and yogurt. Serve it with a salad of mixed greens, including shredded spinach, and dry white wine or chilled beer.

1 cup plain low-fat yogurt
2 large cloves garlic, minced
1/2 teaspoon salt, divided
2 tablespoons olive oil
4 medium onions, chopped fine
6 medium tomatoes, peeled and chopped
1 tablespoon chopped fresh basil *or* 1 teaspoon dried basil
1/4 teaspoon freshly ground black pepper
1 pound whole wheat or imported semolina spaghetti
2 cans (6 1/2 ounces each) water-packed chunk light tuna, drained and flaked
Parsley, for garnish

In a small bowl blend the yogurt, garlic, and 1/4 teaspoon of the salt; set aside.

In a medium saucepan over medium heat, warm the oil. Sauté the onions until they are soft but not browned. Add the tomatoes, the remaining 1/4 teaspoon salt, basil, and ground pepper; simmer for 20 minutes.

While the sauce is cooking, cook the spaghetti until al dente (see page 46). Drain and pour into a large bowl or spaghetti plate.

Stir the tuna into the tomato sauce, then mix the sauce into the pasta, stirring until all the pasta is coated with sauce. Pour the reserved yogurt mixture over the top or drizzle a little over each portion. Garnish with the parsley and serve.

Serves 6.

Tuna and Couscous Niçoise

The garlic and olives give this dish its name. If you can't find Niçoise olives (French olives, tiny and dark brown), use Greek black olives. Serve with chunks of French bread and chilled beer.

1 1/4 cups Chicken Stock (page 146)
1/4 teaspoon salt
2 large cloves garlic, minced
1 teaspoon olive oil
1 1/2 cups medium-grain couscous
2 cups cut-up fresh green beans (1-inch pieces)
1 can (6 1/2 ounces) chunk tuna in water, drained and flaked
2 large tomatoes, peeled and chopped fine
1/4 cup Niçoise olives, pitted and sliced
8 large leaves fresh basil, julienned
1 tablespoon coarsely chopped parsley
1 tablespoon white wine vinegar, preferably tarragon
1/4 teaspoon freshly ground black pepper

In a stove-top casserole with a tight-fitting lid, combine the stock, salt, garlic, and oil and bring to a boil over high heat. Stir in the couscous and remove from the heat. Cover and let stand for 5 minutes.

Meanwhile, cook the beans until they are crisp-tender. Uncover the casserole and fluff the couscous with a fork until the grains are separate. Stir in the beans, tuna, tomatoes, olives, basil, parsley, vinegar, and ground pepper. Heat until warmed through. Serve at once.

Serves 6.

Variation
Tuna and Couscous Salad. Stir in 1 medium green bell pepper, sliced fine; increase the vinegar to 2 tablespoons. Serve at room temperature or chilled over a bed of leafy salad greens.

Scallops Stir-fried with Fresh Ginger & Vegetables

Here is a fresh-tasting, pretty Asian dish, very quickly made. Serve it over mounds of hot short-grain rice, preferably brown (see the Appendix for cooking instructions).

3 teaspoons canola oil, divided
1-inch piece fresh ginger, peeled and minced
1 large clove garlic, minced
1 1/2 cups (about 4 ounces) snow peas cut in half, ends trimmed
1 cup thinly sliced carrot
1 tablespoon low-sodium soy sauce
2 teaspoons cornstarch
1 pound fresh sea scallops
1/2 cup diagonally sliced green onion
4 cups hot cooked short-grain brown rice

In a sauté pan over medium-high heat, warm 2 teaspoons of the oil. Add the fresh ginger and garlic and stir-fry for 30 seconds. Add the snow peas and carrot and stir-fry for 1 minute. Remove the vegetables from the skillet with a slotted spoon. Set aside and keep warm.

In a small bowl combine the soy sauce and cornstarch; set aside.

Add the remaining 1 teaspoon oil to the pan along with the scallops, and stir-fry over medium heat for 3 minutes. Add the reserved vegetables, reserved soy sauce mixture, and green onion. Continue to stir and cook for 1 minute longer. Serve over the hot rice.

Serves 4.

Seafood Linguini with Vegetables

The combination of seafood and pasta has long been a favorite in Mediterranean countries. Here is a change from tomato sauce-based combinations. Serve it with a salad of fresh sliced tomatoes on a bed of mixed greens, lots of crusty garlic bread, and dry white wine.

1 pound linguini or spaghettini
4 quarts water
1 tablespoon olive oil
3 cloves garlic, crushed in a garlic press
1/2 cup chopped celery, including tops
1 medium onion, chopped
2 tablespoons chopped parsley
3 dozen uncooked clams in the shell, well washed
1/2 pound uncooked shrimp, shelled and deveined
1/2 pound bay scallops
1/2 pound fresh mushrooms, sliced
1 1/2 cups tiny peas, fresh, or frozen and defrosted
1/2 cup dry white wine
1/4 cup shredded Parmesan or Asiago cheese

In a large pot over high heat, cook the pasta in the water until al dente. Drain, rinse in hot water, and keep warm.

Meanwhile, in a large saucepan over medium heat, warm the oil. Sauté the garlic, celery, onion, and parsley. Add the clams; when they start to open, add the shrimp, scallops, mushrooms, and peas. Simmer until the shrimp are pink and the clams are fully open. Be careful not to overcook. Stir in the white wine and heat through.

Transfer the pasta to a large serving bowl and top with the seafood mixture. Sprinkle with the cheese, mix well, and serve on warmed plates.

Serves 6 generously.

Shrimp Sauté with Indian Spices

This quickly prepared meal combines several interesting sweet and hot spices and their fragrances. Basmati rice, also fragrant, makes the perfect accompaniment. Serve this dish with a slightly rich, fruity white wine.

1 1/2 cups brown basmati rice
3 to 3 1/2 cups boiling water
1 teaspoon salt
1/2 teaspoon cumin seeds
1/4 teaspoon coriander seeds
1 tablespoon canola oil
1 1/2 pounds large shrimp, peeled and deveined
1/8 teaspoon red pepper flakes
1/4 teaspoon freshly ground white pepper
1 shallot *or* 2 green onions, minced
5 cloves garlic, minced
1-inch piece fresh ginger, peeled and minced
2 teaspoons curry powder
1 can (28 ounces) whole tomatoes, chopped, with juice
1 red bell pepper, sliced thin
1 green bell pepper, sliced thin
1 small zucchini, cut into sticks 1/2 inch by 2 1/2 inches
1/2 cup chopped cilantro or flat-leaf (Italian) parsley
1 tablespoon lemon juice

In a medium saucepan over medium-high heat, combine the rice, boiling water, and 3/4 teaspoon of the salt; cook until the rice is done (about 45 minutes). Keep warm.

In a small skillet over medium-high heat, toast the cumin and coriander seeds until fragrant (30 to 40 seconds), shaking the pan. Let cool, then crush with a mortar and pestle and set aside.

In a large sauté pan or heavy skillet over medium-high heat, warm the oil. Add the shrimp and red pepper flakes; sauté until the shrimp turn bright pink (2 to 3 minutes). With a slotted spoon transfer the shrimp to a plate and season with the remaining 1/4 teaspoon salt and the ground pepper. Set aside.

Add the shallot, garlic, fresh ginger, curry, and reserved crushed seeds to the skillet.

Cook, stirring, until the shallot is lightly browned (about 1 minute). Stir in the tomatoes, bell peppers, and zucchini. Cook, stirring often, until the sauce thickens somewhat (8 to 10 minutes). Add the reserved shrimp, the cilantro, and lemon juice and heat through. Serve over the reserved hot rice.

Serves 6.

Mussels with Rice Pilaf

This dish combines several cooking traditions, in keeping with the international exchange of ideas that enhances today's cooking. Serve this simple dish with crusty French bread and a good white wine.

1 tablespoon olive oil
1 cup chopped onion
3 cloves garlic, minced
1 cup long-grain white or basmati rice
1 teaspoon dried oregano
1/2 teaspoon salt
1/4 teaspoon freshly ground white pepper
2 cups Chicken Stock (page 146) or Fish Stock (page 146)
24 mussels, scrubbed and debearded
1 large carrot, julienned
1 cup snow peas cut in half, ends trimmed

    In a large sauté pan over medium heat, warm the oil. Sauté the onion and garlic for about 5 minutes. Add the rice, oregano, salt, and ground pepper and sauté for 3 minutes more. Pour in the stock and bring to a boil. Reduce the heat, cover, and simmer for 20 minutes.

    Add the mussels and carrot. Loosely cover the pan and continue cooking. When the mussels begin to open, add the snow peas. Cover and simmer until the mussels are completely open (about 6 minutes). Be careful not to overcook. Discard any mussels that don't open. Serve immediately.

Serves 4.

Vegetable Medley with Mozzarella Topping

This is an American adaptation of the German *Allerei*. Here is a place to use fresh herbs, if you have them in your garden. Serve thick slices of rye or whole wheat bread and chilled beer or hearty red wine.

1 tablespoon olive oil
1 large onion, sliced thin
2 red bell peppers, cut in half crosswise, then into thin lengthwise strips
2 medium potatoes, halved, then sliced thin
1 cup sliced green beans
2 small to medium zucchini (about 3/4 pound total), cut into thin rounds
2 medium tomatoes, cut into 1-inch cubes
1 tablespoon minced fresh summer savory or lemon thyme *or* 1 teaspoon dried winter savory or thyme
1/2 teaspoon salt
1/2 teaspoon freshly ground white pepper
1/4 cup whole wheat bread crumbs, toasted, or unsweetened crunchy whole wheat cereal, such as Kellogg's Nutrigrain
1 cup shredded part-skim mozzarella cheese

    In a large skillet with a lid, warm the oil over medium heat. Saute the onion for 1 minute, then add the bell peppers and cook for about 1 minute longer. Add the potatoes and beans and cook, stirring, for about 5 minutes. Stir in the zucchini, tomatoes, savory, salt, and ground pepper. Cover closely and cook, stirring occasionally, for about 10 minutes.

    Remove the pan from the heat. Combine the bread crumbs and cheese; sprinkle over the vegetables. Cover and let the cheese melt, or place the skillet under the broiler until the cheese is lightly browned (about 5 minutes). Serve hot.

Serves 4 to 6.

Indonesian Stir-fry

This dish is hot, so be forewarned. Serve it with a salad of romaine and orange slices with Creamy Orange Dressing (page 150) and chilled medium-dry white wine.

1 tablespoon peanut oil
1 hot green chile, seeded and minced
2 tablespoons minced peeled fresh ginger
4 cloves garlic, minced
1 red bell pepper, cut into strips
1 green bell pepper, cut into strips
1 cup thinly sliced green onion
2 celery stalks, cut into thin diagonal slices
1/2 cup thinly sliced fresh mushrooms
3/4 cup broccoli florets
3/4 cup sliced cauliflower florets
2 cups Vegetable Stock (page 147)
1/2 cup unsalted peanut butter
2 tablespoons low-sodium soy sauce
1 tablespoon lemon juice
1 teaspoon honey
1/2 teaspoon red pepper flakes
2 cups cubed firm tofu (1/2-inch pieces)
3 to 4 cups hot cooked short-grain rice

In a large skillet over medium heat, warm the oil. Sauté the chile, fresh ginger, and garlic for 5 minutes. Add the bell peppers, green onion, celery, mushrooms, broccoli, and cauliflower; stir to combine.

Add 1 cup of the stock, stirring to deglaze the pan. In a 2-cup measure combine the remaining 1 cup stock, peanut butter, soy sauce, lemon juice, honey, and pepper flakes; add to the pan. Cook over medium heat, stirring constantly, until the sauce thickens and begins to simmer; then reduce the heat and add the tofu. Cover and cook until the vegetables are crisp-tender (4 to 5 minutes). Serve over the hot rice.

Serves 6.

Variation

Vietnamese Stir-fry. Omit the chile, peanut butter, lemon juice, honey, and red pepper flakes. Use only 1 cup stock and season it with 1 tablespoon rice vinegar, 1/2 teaspoon ground cumin, and 3 tablespoons minced cilantro.

Vegetable-topped Crisp Noodles

Although this Chinese dish is more complicated than many given here, it is fun and different and well worth the extra effort.

10 to 12 ounces Asian rice noodles
3 tablespoons canola oil, divided
1/2 teaspoon salt
1 large clove garlic, minced
1 medium onion, minced
2 tablespoons minced peeled fresh ginger
2 stalks celery, cut into thin diagonal slices
2 medium carrots, cut into thin diagonal slices
1 green or red bell pepper, cut into 1/4-inch strips
1 1/2 cups sliced broccoli florets and stems, kept separate, with stems cut into 1/4-inch slices
1/4 pound fresh mushrooms, sliced
3 tablespoons water
3 tablespoons cornstarch
2 tablespoons low-sodium soy sauce
1/8 teaspoon cayenne pepper
1/4 cup dry sherry
2 1/2 cups Root Vegetable Stock (147)
1 pound firm tofu, drained and cut into 3/4-inch cubes

Cook the noodles according to package directions, then drain and toss with 1 tablespoon of the oil and the salt. Set aside.

Place a 14-inch pizza pan or a 15- by 10-inch baking sheet with a rim in a 500 degree F oven. When the pan is very hot, pour in 1 tablespoon of the oil and tilt to coat. Spread the cooked noodles evenly in the pan and bake uncovered on the bottom rack of the oven until golden (25 to 30 minutes).

About 10 minutes before the noodles are done, heat the remaining 1 tablespoon oil in a wok or a large sauté pan over medium-high heat. Add the garlic, onion, fresh ginger, celery, carrots, bell pepper, and broccoli stems and stir-fry for 2 minutes. Reduce the heat to medium and add the water. Cover and cook for 3 minutes, stirring often. Add the broccoli florets and mushrooms and stir-fry for 1 minute.

Combine the water, cornstarch, soy sauce, cayenne, sherry, and stock; stir into the pan along with the tofu. Cook until the sauce boils and thickens.

To serve, loosen the crisp noodles from the pan and slide them onto a cutting board. Cut into 6 wedges or rectangles, transfer to individual plates, and top with the vegetables and sauce.

Serves 6.

Spirals with Fresh Tomatoes, Broccoli, & Pesto

The wonderful Italian mixture called pesto has become very popular in this country. Serve this, as well as the other pasta dishes here, with Simple Garlic Bread (page 152) or crusty Italian bread, and hearty Italian red wine.

1 pound broccoli, florets separated, stems cut crosswise into 1/2-inch slices
1 pound spirals or shell pasta, preferably colored vegetable pasta
1 tablespoon olive oil
1 large clove garlic, minced
2 medium tomatoes, cut into 1-inch chunks
1/2 teaspoon freshly ground black pepper
2/3 cup Pesto (page 149), diluted with 1/4 cup boiling water
1/4 cup freshly grated Parmesan or Sap Sago cheese

In a large pot over high heat, bring 2 quarts water to a boil. Cook the broccoli for 4 minutes. Remove it with a slotted spoon and keep warm.

In the same pot, add 2 more quarts water, bring it to a rolling boil, and cook the pasta until al dente.

Meanwhile, in a large skillet over medium heat, warm the oil. Add the garlic and cook until brown. Add the cooked broccoli, tossing gently until it is heated through. Add the tomatoes and ground pepper; remove from the heat, and cover.

Drain the pasta and arrange it in a large, shallow, heated dish. Pour the reserved broccoli and tomatoes over the top. Top with the diluted Pesto and toss gently. Pass the cheese to sprinkle over individual portions.

Linguini with Broccoli, Cauliflower, & Mushrooms

This pasta dish, an adaptation of a much weightier version, provides a change from the usual tomato sauces. Purists may take issue with the use of farmer cheese, but the result is very good indeed.

1 cup farmer cheese
1/4 cup grated Romano or Sap Sago cheese
1 medium head cauliflower, cut into florets
1 medium bunch broccoli, cut into florets
2 tablespoons olive oil
6 cloves garlic, sliced thin
1 pound fresh mushrooms, sliced thick
3/4 teaspoon salt
1/2 teaspoon cayenne pepper
1 pound linguini

Combine the farmer and Romano cheeses and set aside. In a large pot of boiling lightly salted water, cook the cauliflower and broccoli for about 5 minutes. Remove the vegetables with a slotted spoon, reserving the liquid for cooking the linguini.

In a large skillet over medium heat, warm the oil. Lightly brown the garlic; stir in the mushrooms, salt, and cayenne; sauté for about 5 minutes.

Bring the vegetable cooking water to a rapid boil, adding enough water to make 4 quarts. Add the linguini, stir well to prevent sticking, and cook until al dente (about 10 minutes; see page 46).

Meanwhile, stir the reserved broccoli and cauliflower into the garlic and mushrooms. Cover and continue cooking until the vegetables are just tender. Drain the pasta, stir into the vegetables, and heat thoroughly. Top with the reserved cheese mixture and serve immediately.

Serves 8.

Pasta Primavera

This dish, a family favorite, is one of the prettiest you can serve. Feel free to vary the vegetables and use whatever you have on hand (mushrooms, fresh beans, asparagus, and celery are all possibilities). Just be sure to maintain a range of colors. If you use green beans, carrots, celery, broccoli, or asparagus—and I often do—steam them briefly before adding to the pan. Here is an appropriate meal for family participation, since each person can prepare a vegetable or two.

1 pound whole wheat spaghetti or flat spinach
   pasta
1/3 cup pine nuts
1 1/2 cups fresh broccoli cut into small pieces
1 cup julienned or thinly sliced carrot
1 tablespoon vegetable oil
1 large clove garlic, chopped fine
4 large green onions, cut into 1 1/2-inch slices
2 tablespoons chopped fresh basil *or* 2 teaspoons
   dried basil
1 tablespoon chopped fresh oregano *or* 1 teaspoon dried oregano
1/2 large green bell pepper, halved and julienned
1/2 red bell pepper, halved and julienned
1 cup snow peas cut in half, ends trimmed
1 cup julienned zucchini
2 large fresh tomatoes, cut into 1-inch cubes
1/4 cup minced parsley
1/2 cup plain low-fat yogurt
1/2 cup grated Parmesan cheese

Cook the spaghetti in 4 quarts rapidly boiling water until al dente (see page 46). Drain and set aside, keeping it warm. Toast the pine nuts in a 350 degree F oven until lightly browned; set aside. Steam the broccoli and carrot until crisp-tender; set aside.

In a large sauté pan over medium heat, warm the olive oil. Sauté the garlic, green onions, basil, oregano, bell peppers, snow peas, and zucchini until the vegetables are slightly cooked but still crisp. Add the tomatoes, parsley, yogurt, and steamed broccoli and carrot; cook until heated thoroughly.

Add the reserved spaghetti, reserved pine nuts, reserved broccoli and carrot, and the Parmesan cheese; toss gently to mix. Serve hot.

Serves 6 to 8.

Garden Vegetable Curry

Hot and spicy describes this dish from Pakistan. The addition of yogurt at the end of cooking will tame some of the fire. Serve it with a green salad topped with citrus slices and Creamy Orange Dressing (page 150), and chilled beer.

1 tablespoon vegetable oil
4 cloves garlic, minced
1 tablespoon minced peeled fresh ginger
1 teaspoon red pepper flakes
1 teaspoon ground turmeric
1 teaspoon fennel seeds
1 teaspoon ground coriander
1/4 teaspoon ground cumin
2 medium onions, chopped coarsely
2 medium potatoes, cut into 1/2-inch cubes
1 cup diced carrot
1 cup chopped red bell pepper
1 cup chopped green bell pepper
4 medium tomatoes, chopped
3 cups cauliflower florets
1 teaspoon salt
1/4 cup water
2 cups fresh or frozen peas
1 cup plain nonfat yogurt
3 cups hot cooked brown rice
1/4 cup chopped cilantro or parsley

In a large sauté pan over medium heat, warm the oil. Add the garlic, fresh ginger, pepper flakes, turmeric, fennel, coriander, and cumin; sauté until fragrant (about 20 seconds). Reduce the heat to low and add the onions. Cook, stirring, until soft (about 4 minutes).

Add the potatoes, carrots, bell peppers, tomatoes, cauliflower, and salt. Stir to combine; then add the water and bring to a boil, stirring constantly. Reduce the heat, cover, and simmer until the vege-

tables are crisp-tender (about 10 minutes). Add the peas; cover and cook until they are tender (2 to 3 minutes). Remove from the heat and stir in the yogurt.

Serve by mounding the rice and vegetables side by side; garnish with the chopped cilantro.

Serves 6 to 8.

Variation

Tofu and Vegetable Curry. Add 1 pound firm tofu, cut into 1-inch cubes, with the vegetables and proceed as above. Serves 8.

Bulgur and Chick-peas

This is a popular Middle Eastern dish that is easy to make. It is best to start with dried chick-peas that you have soaked and cooked yourself ahead of time (see the Appendix). Serve with toasted pita bread and hearty red wine.

1 tablespoon olive oil
1 1/4 cups uncooked medium bulgur
1 medium onion, chopped
1 clove garlic, minced
1 teaspoon ground cumin
2 1/2 cups Root Vegetable Stock (page 147)
1/2 teaspoon dried oregano
1/2 teaspoon dried dill weed
1/2 teaspoon salt
1/2 teaspoon freshly ground black pepper
3/4 cup cooked chick-peas or canned chick-peas, rinsed and drained
1 medium zucchini, quartered and sliced thin
1 cup plain nonfat yogurt

In a large saucepan or stove-top casserole with a lid, warm the oil over medium heat. Sauté the bulgur until it is slightly browned (about 5 minutes). Add the onion, garlic, and cumin and sauté, stirring, for another 5 minutes. Stir in the stock, oregano, dill, salt, and ground pepper. Bring to a boil, then reduce the heat, cover, and simmer until the stock is absorbed (about 20 minutes).

Stir in the chick-peas and zucchini; cover and cook for 5 minutes. Stir in the yogurt and heat thoroughly. Serve hot.

Serves 6.

Variations

Bulgur and Lentils. Substitute 3/4 cup cooked lentils for the chick-peas; sauté one small green bell pepper with the onion and garlic. Substitute 1/2 teaspoon ground allspice for the oregano and dill. Stir in 2 teaspoons grated lemon zest with the yogurt. Garnish with chopped parsley, if desired.

Pilaf with Chick-peas. Substitute long-grain brown rice for the bulgur and stir in 1 package (10 ounces) frozen chopped spinach (thawed) and 1/4 cup quick-cooking rolled oats with the chick-peas. Add more liquid if needed.

Risotto Pomodoro con le zucchine

No discourse on international food would be complete without some comments on risotto. This northern Italian dish is made with *arborio*, a short-grain Italian white rice; it is cooked with the liquid added in stages until the rice reaches a creamy yet al dente consistency. The Italians would serve this as a first course before the veal, chicken, or roast. This particular version can stand by itself, or you can add chopped ham or sweet sausage, or strips of chicken breast (about 1/2 pound in all cases). Accompany it with a light mixed green salad and dry white wine.

2 tablespoons olive oil, divided
3 tablespoons coarsely chopped onion
3 large cloves garlic, minced
4 medium *or* 6 small zucchini, sliced into 1/2-inch-thick rounds
Pinch salt
4 1/2 to 5 cups Vegetable Stock (page 147)
1 1/2 cups uncooked arborio or other short-grain white rice
3 medium tomatoes, chopped
Freshly ground black pepper, to taste
1 tablespoon minced flat-leaf (Italian) parsley
3 tablespoons grated Parmesan cheese, plus more for serving

In a large Dutch oven or heavy stove-top casserole with a lid, warm 1 tablespoon of the oil over medium-high heat. Sauté the onion until it becomes translucent. Add the garlic; as soon as it colors slightly, stir in the zucchini. Reduce the heat to medium-low, add the salt, and cook until the zucchini reaches a rich golden color (about 20 minutes).

Meanwhile, in a large saucepan over medium-low heat, warm the stock to a slow, steady simmer.

Add the remaining 1 tablespoon oil to the zucchini in the Dutch oven and increase the heat to high.

When the zucchini begins to bubble, add the rice and stir until it is well coated. Sauté lightly for about 1 minute, then reduce the heat to medium-low and add 1/2 cup of the simmering stock. Stir while cooking until the rice absorbs the liquid. When the rice dries out, add another 1/2 cup stock and continue to stir as the rice cooks. Stir in the tomatoes.

You must be tireless in your stirring of the rice mixture, always loosening the rice from the entire bottom surface of the pot. Keep adding liquid as the rice dries out, but be patient and don't drown the rice. Be sure that the cooking heat is right—hot enough to reduce the liquid but slow enough for the rice to cook evenly.

When the rice is done, taste for seasoning. Remember that the Parmesan that you will be adding is salty. Turn off the heat, grind a few turns of the pepper mill over everything, and add the minced parsley and Parmesan; mix thoroughly. Serve immediately with more freshly grated Parmesan on the side.

Serves 4.

Variations

Risotto Primavera. About 10 minutes before the rice is done, stir in 1 small carrot, cut into 1/4-inch dice; 1 cup asparagus pieces (1 1/2-inch pieces), blanched; 1 cup sugar snap peas cut in half, strings and stems removed, blanched; and 1 cup thinly sliced spinach leaves, rinsed. Stir well. Serves 6.

Risotto with Salmon and Peas. Omit the zucchini. Add the rice to the pot after you have sautéed the onion and garlic. With the last addition of liquid, stir in 12 ounces salmon fillet, cut into cubes, and 2 cups fresh or frozen peas. Cook until the liquid is absorbed and the peas are cooked. Serves 4.

Stews

Although we are inclined to think of stews as hearty country fare, there are many sophisticated examples from the most elegant cuisines. Almost every cooking tradition throughout the world has a selection of stews, many of which I have included. The method here is the slow cooking of a combination of ingredients, with ample time given to not only the cooking of the food but the blending of flavors.

Be sure to have a good supply of hearty bread on hand to soak up the wonderful stew juices left on the plate.

Beef with Tomatoes and Rice, Catalan Style

This dish comes from the western Mediterranean corner of France. It is perfect with a mixed green salad, whole-grain French bread, and young red wine.

2 strips turkey bacon
1 tablespoon olive oil
1 1/2 pounds lean top round, all visible fat removed, cut into 1-inch cubes
1 1/2 cups sliced onion
1 cup long-grain white rice
1/2 cup water
1/2 cup dry white wine
3 cups Beef Stock (page 146), or as needed
Salt, to taste
2 cups thinly sliced carrot
1 cup thinly sliced celery
1/4 teaspoon freshly ground black pepper
2 large cloves garlic, crushed in a garlic press
1 teaspoon dried thyme
1 bay leaf, crumbled
1 1/2 cups chopped ripe tomato
1/2 cup grated Parmesan cheese

In a heavy Dutch oven with a lid, fry the bacon over medium heat until just cooked. Drain and cut into 1-inch pieces. Set aside.

Pour off any excess fat from the pot, add the oil, and warm it over medium-high heat. Add the meat and cook it until browned. Reduce the heat to medium; stir in the onion and brown it slightly. Remove the meat and onion to a large platter.

In the oil in the same pot, add the rice and cook, stirring, over medium heat until it turns a milky color (about 3 minutes). Spoon the rice into a bowl and set aside.

Pour any remaining oil out of the pot; add the water and stir for a moment to dissolve the juices. Add the wine, stir, then return the meat and onion to the pot. Pour in the stock almost to the height of the meat and salt it lightly. Add the carrot, celery, ground pepper, garlic, thyme, bay leaf, and reserved bacon. Bring to a simmer, cover tightly, and simmer slowly for 1 hour.

Stir in the chopped tomato and simmer until the meat is fork-tender (1 hour or more). Drain off the cooking liquid and add stock or water to make 2 1/2 cups. Return the liquid to the pot and bring to a boil. Stir in the reserved rice, cover, and simmer for about 20 minutes without stirring. The rice should be tender and have absorbed almost all the liquid. Taste and correct the seasoning. Just before serving, fold in the grated cheese. Serve from the casserole.

Serves 6.

Variation

Beef and Bean Stew, Arabian Style. Omit the celery and cheese. Stir in 2 cups cooked navy beans and 1/4 teaspoon ground cinnamon with the tomato. Serves 8.

Easy Beef Stew, Italian Style

This adaptation of a popular beef stew (called *Manzo brasato* in Italy) combines the traditional vegetables, which are easily prepared in a food processor for a *soffritto*, a mixture of chopped vegetables cooked in oil and reduced to a thick, glazed sauce. Serve this dish with a salad of sliced raw mushrooms and green onion tops on a bed of greens, dressed with garlic, lemon, and olive oil, and Simple Garlic Bread (page 152).

All-purpose flour, for dusting meat
1 pound lean top round, all visible fat removed, cut into 1-inch cubes
1 tablespoon olive oil
1 tablespoon Italian Herb Blend (page 150)
1 large clove garlic, minced
1/2 teaspoon salt
1/2 teaspoon freshly ground black pepper
1/2 cup coarsely chopped onion
1/2 cup coarsely chopped carrot
1/2 cup coarsely chopped celery
1/4 cup dry red wine
2 cups Beef Stock (page 146)
3 medium potatoes, halved lengthwise, then sliced
1 can (28 ounces) tomatoes, coarsely chopped, with juice
1 bay leaf

Sprinkle the flour over the meat. In a heavy Dutch oven with a lid, warm the oil over medium-high heat. Add the beef and cook until it is brown and crusty on all sides. Remove to a plate and set aside.

Add the herb blend, garlic, salt, and ground pepper to the pot; cook for several minutes. Add the onion, carrot, and celery; cook, stirring, until the vegetables soften and become thick and slightly glazed (about 8 minutes). This is the *soffritto*.

Reduce the heat to medium-low; add the wine and stir to deglaze the pot. Add the stock, reserved beef, potatoes, tomatoes, and bay leaf. Increase the heat to high and bring the stew to a boil, then reduce the heat to low, cover the pot tightly, and simmer until the meat is tender (about 2 hours). Discard the bay leaf and serve.

Serves 6.

Variations

Ragoût de Boeuf Bordelaise. Substitute 1 teaspoon dried thyme and 1/4 teaspoon ground cloves for the Italian Herb Blend. Omit the celery. Fifteen minutes before serving, add 12 fresh mushrooms, sliced and sautéed, and 1 cup peas. Heat thoroughly.

Beef Stew, Pizza Style. Omit the potatoes. About 15 minutes before serving, sprinkle 2 ounces shredded part-skim mozzarella cheese over the top. Cover and cook until the cheese has melted. Serve over hot cooked pasta or brown rice.

Chili con Carne

This dish of well-seasoned beef with chiles is one of the most famous dishes of Texas, although it is found all over the United States in different forms. Recipes are available for chili with chicken (see the variation below) and for vegetarian versions, that is, without carne (page 94). This adaptation with lots of vegetables is an easy dish, hearty and very well flavored. You can vary the amount of heat by adjusting the amount (and strength) of the chili powder and fresh chopped chiles. This dish is traditionally served with steamed white rice and chilled beer.

1 pound lean ground beef
1 cup chopped onion
2 cloves garlic, minced
3 cups water
2 cups thinly sliced zucchini
2 cups sliced fresh mushrooms
3/4 cup thinly sliced carrot
1/2 cup chopped green bell pepper
1 can (4 ounces) chopped green chiles, undrained
1/3 cup Crushed Tomatoes (page 148) or tomato paste
1 1/2 tablespoons chili powder
1/2 teaspoon salt
1 teaspoon dried oregano
1/2 teaspoon ground cumin
1/4 teaspoon freshly ground black pepper
1 can (28 ounces) tomatoes, chopped, with juice
1 can (19 ounces) red kidney beans, rinsed and drained

In a large Dutch oven over medium heat, cook the meat with the onion and garlic until browned, stirring to crumble. Drain and pat dry, wiping drippings from the pan with a paper towel.

Return the meat to the pan. Add the remaining ingredients and bring to a boil. Reduce the heat and simmer, uncovered, for 1 hour, stirring occasionally. Serve steaming hot.

Serves 8.

Variations

High-fiber Chili. Stir in 1 cup Kellogg's All-Bran cereal with the other ingredients.

Chicken Chili. Substitute 1 pound skinned, boned chicken breast, diced, for the ground beef. Sauté it with the onion and garlic in 1 tablespoon canola oil. Substitute 2 cups Chicken Stock (page 146) for 2 cups of the water. Substitute canned chick-peas or cannellini beans for the kidney beans. Add 1 teaspoon ground coriander with the other seasonings.

Slender Blanquette de Veau

I can remember eating this dish as a student in Paris. It was very rich, with a cream sauce fortified with egg yolks. Here is an adaptation for today's healthier palate. This dish is traditionally served with egg noodles or white rice. I find brown rice more appealing, as it adds flavor and color. Serve the stew with a salad of tender head lettuce and Light Herb Dressing (page 149) and, of course, French bread.

1 teaspoon butter or light margarine
2 pounds lean boneless veal, all visible fat removed, cut into 1-inch cubes
3 bay leaves
2 teaspoons celery salt
1 teaspoon dried thyme
1/2 teaspoon freshly ground white pepper
2 cups Chicken Stock (page 146)
1 1/2 pounds small white onions
1/2 pound fresh mushrooms, sliced
1 cup fresh or frozen tiny peas
1/4 cup evaporated skimmed milk
3 tablespoons chopped parsley
3 cups hot cooked long-grain brown rice

In a heavy Dutch oven over medium heat, melt the butter. Sauté the veal until lightly browned. Combine the bay leaves, celery salt, thyme, ground pepper, and stock. Pour over the veal. Reduce the heat to the lowest setting, cover, and simmer for 1 hour.

Skim off any scum that has formed. Place the onions on top of the meat. Cover and simmer until the veal and onions are tender (about 45 minutes).

Stir in the mushrooms, peas, and evaporated milk. Cover and simmer for 10 minutes. Discard the bay leaves. Sprinkle with the parsley and serve over the hot rice.

Serves 6.

Variation
Veal in Wine. Substitute 1/4 cup dry sherry for the evaporated milk, adding it with the onions.

Lemony Veal Stew

This elegant version of a German *Kalbsragout* would be served with a *Kopfsalat*, that is, whole Boston lettuce leaves with Light Herb Dressing (page 149), and a chilled medium-dry white wine.

1 1/2 pounds boneless veal, all visible fat removed, cut into 1-inch cubes
All-purpose flour, for dredging the meat
1/2 teaspoon salt
1/2 teaspoon freshly ground white pepper
1 tablespoon canola oil
2 large carrots, diced
2 large onions, chopped
Butter, if needed
1/2 teaspoon dried winter savory
4 medium potatoes, cubed
2 cups cut green beans (1-inch pieces)
2 teaspoons grated lemon zest
Juice of 2 lemons
Pinch ground nutmeg

Pat the veal cubes dry, then dredge them in the flour seasoned with the salt and ground pepper. In a stove-top casserole with a lid, warm the oil over medium heat. Sauté the carrots and onions for 5 minutes. Push them aside, add the floured veal cubes, and brown on all sides, adding a bit of butter if needed.

Sprinkle the savory over the veal and add enough water to show through the top of the stew. Cover and cook very slowly for 1 1/2 hours. Add the potatoes and beans and continue to cook slowly until the vegetables are tender (about 20 minutes), adding more water during the cooking, if needed. Stir in the lemon zest, lemon juice, and nutmeg and heat thoroughly. Serve hot.

Serves 6.

Variation

Savory Veal Stew. Omit the onions, green beans, and winter savory. Instead use 3 leeks, cut into 3-inch pieces; 1 small head cabbage, halved and sliced; 2 bay leaves; 1 teaspoon caraway seeds; and 1 teaspoon fennel seeds.

Uruguayan Carbonada

Here is an unusual combination of wholesome ingredients, especially the yellow vegetables. Serve this with plenty of hearty whole wheat bread to soak up the sauce and well-chilled beer.

1 tablespoon canola oil
2 large cloves garlic, chopped
1 medium onion, chopped
1 pound boneless veal, all visible fat removed, cut into 1-inch cubes
2 tomatoes, cubed
1 medium potato, diced
1 hubbard or butternut squash, peeled and diced
1 medium to large sweet potato, peeled and diced
1 cup fresh corn kernels, cut from the cob
1 teaspoon dried thyme
1 teaspoon dried summer savory
1/2 teaspoon salt
1/2 teaspoon freshly ground white pepper
3 cups Root Vegetable Stock (page 147), or more if needed
1 cup long-grain white rice
2 small tart apples, diced

In a heavy Dutch oven or flameproof casserole with a lid, warm the oil over medium heat. Sauté the garlic and onion until lightly browned. Add the veal and brown it.

Add the tomatoes, potato, squash, sweet potato, corn, thyme, savory, salt, ground pepper, and stock. Bring to a boil; then reduce the heat, cover, and simmer until almost done (about 1 1/2 hours).

Add the rice and apples and simmer, covered, until the rice is cooked (about 25 minutes). Add more stock if necessary; the consistency should be slightly less liquid than a thick soup. Serve hot.

Serves 6.

Variation

Carbonada in a Pumpkin. After you have added the vegetables, seasonings, and stock and brought the stew to a boil, you can bake it in a large pumpkin, which you have hollowed out, removing all seeds and pith. Place the filled pumpkin in a baking dish and cover it with the pumpkin top (if the top has a stem, cover it with foil so it won't burn). Bake at 350 degrees F until the pumpkin is tender (about 2 hours), adding the rice and apples after the first hour. When serving, scoop out the cooked pumpkin along with the filling.

Cassoulet, Slender Style

The traditional version of this dish takes several days to cook and calls for goose breast, not to mention pork rind, loin, and sausage. This version takes less time and eliminates many of the fat-filled ingredients, yet almost all the flavor and special qualities of the dish remain. Keep in mind that the beans must soak overnight, and that the dish is eaten the second day. Serve it with a green salad (try fresh green beans, slightly cooked, on a bed of mixed greens), hearty red wine or chilled beer, and lots of whole-grain French bread.

1/2 pound dried navy beans
4 slices turkey bacon
1 pound lean stewing lamb, all visible fat removed, cut into 1-inch cubes *or* 2 cups leftover roast lamb
1/4 pound mild Italian turkey sausage, cut into small pieces
1 large onion, chopped
1 large clove garlic, sliced thin
2 cups chopped tomato *or* 1 can (16 ounces) whole tomatoes, chopped, with juice
1 bay leaf
1/2 teaspoon dried thyme
1/2 teaspoon dried basil
1/2 teaspoon salt
1/2 teaspoon freshly ground black pepper
3 cups hot cooked long-grain brown rice

Pour boiling water over the beans and let them soak overnight. Drain; then pour fresh water over to cover and simmer until done (about 1 hour). Drain, reserving the liquid, and set aside.

In a large stove-top casserole, fry the bacon until crisp. Drain on paper towels, crumble, and set aside.

Drain the fat from the casserole and sauté the lamb until browned. Add the lamb to the beans.

Sauté the sausage, onion, and garlic until browned. Drain off the fat. Then add the tomato, bay leaf, thyme, and basil and stir well. Season with the salt and ground pepper and cook for about 1 hour, adding some of the bean liquid, if necessary. Mix in the reserved lamb, cooked beans, and bacon. Chill overnight.

The next day, add the remaining bean liquid to the casserole and cook the cassoulet slowly, for 3 to 4 hours, over low heat. Serve over the hot rice.

Serves 4 to 6.

Lamb and Potatoes, Provençal Style

This stew—one of my favorite lamb dishes—is infinitely quicker and easier than a cassoulet, and equally good. Serve it with mixed greens and Creamy Vinaigrette (page 149) and hearty red wine.

1 tablespoon olive oil
1 pound stewing lamb, all visible fat removed, cut into small chunks
2 large onions, sliced
2 cloves garlic, chopped
3 teaspoons Herbes de Provence (page 150) *or* 2 teaspoons dried basil, divided
1/2 teaspoon salt, divided
1/2 teaspoon freshly ground black pepper
3 medium potatoes, halved, then sliced thin
1/4 cup water
4 small zucchini, sliced thin
3 cups chopped tomato

In a large stove-top casserole with a lid, warm the oil over medium-high heat. Brown the lamb thoroughly. Reduce the heat to medium, add the onions and garlic, and sauté until soft. Stir in 2 teaspoons of the herbs, 1/4 teaspoon of the salt, the ground pepper, potatoes, and the water. Reduce the heat to low, cover, and cook for 20 minutes.

Stir in the zucchini and tomato with the remaining herbs and salt. Cook, stirring occasionally, until the zucchini are translucent and the potatoes are done.

Serves 6.

Variation

Lahem Mashwe. For this Middle Eastern stew, add 3 medium carrots and 3 stalks celery, both sliced thin, along with the potatoes. Instead of the herbs, use 1 teaspoon cumin seeds and 1 tablespoon chopped cilantro. Serves 6 to 8.

New England Pork and Applesauce

This delicious autumn meal provides the pork and applesauce all in one dish. Serve with Triple Wheat Biscuits (page 152) and chilled medium-dry white wine.

2 pounds boneless pork tenderloin, all visible fat removed, cut into chunks
3 cups homemade applesauce, slightly sweetened
1 tablespoon ground cinnamon
2 teaspoons ground nutmeg
1 teaspoon ground cloves
8 small red potatoes
6 carrots, cut into chunks
2 stalks celery, sliced diagonally
2 cups white pearl onions
2 firm tart apples, sliced thin

In a large Dutch oven over medium heat, combine the pork, applesauce, cinnamon, nutmeg, and cloves. Cover tightly and cook for 15 minutes; then reduce the heat and simmer for about 6 hours.

About 1 1/2 hours before serving, add the potatoes, carrots, celery, and onions. Fifteen minutes before serving, add the apple slices.

Serves 6.

Variation

Cranberry-Applesauce Pork. Combine 1 cup whole cranberry sauce, 1/4 cup apricot preserves, and 1/4 cup cranberry juice; add with the vegetables. If desired, instead of the new red potatoes substitute 4 large sweet potatoes, peeled, halved, and sliced thick.

Moroccan Bean Stew

Called *Dfina*, this stew is one of many possible lamb and bean combinations and a favorite in Mediterranean and Middle Eastern cooking. The stew will take some time to prepare (note that the chick-peas and lima beans must soak overnight), but it will fill your kitchen with a wonderful aroma. Serve it with a salad of oranges and red onion slices on greens, garnished with chopped fresh mint, and hearty wheat bread or pita.

1/2 pound dried chick-peas
1/2 pound dried baby lima beans
2 tablespoons olive oil
2 large onions, chopped fine
1 1/2 pounds lean stewing lamb, all visible fat
    removed, cut into chunks
1 teaspoon ground coriander
1 teaspoon ground cumin
1/8 teaspoon ground saffron
24 small new potatoes
2 large carrots, cut into 2-inch pieces
6 cups water
Juice of 1 lemon
Salt and freshly ground black pepper, to taste
2 tablespoons slivered almonds, toasted
2 tablespoons chopped fresh mint

Measure the chick-peas and lima beans into a large bowl, add boiling water to 2 inches above the beans, and soak overnight. Drain and rinse. Set aside.

In a heavy Dutch oven over medium-high heat, warm the oil. Add the onions and sauté until golden. Combine with the chick-peas and beans.

Add the lamb to the pot and sauté until lightly browned. Stir in the coriander, cumin, and saffron; let the spices sizzle for a minute. Then stir in the reserved chick-peas, beans, and onions. Tuck the potatoes and carrots around the other ingredients. Add the water and bring to a simmer. Skim the surface; then cover and place over the lowest heat for 1 1/2 to 2 hours. Stir in the lemon juice and taste. Add the salt and pepper to taste.

Continue to simmer until the liquid has been mostly absorbed (about 2 hours). Sprinkle with the toasted nuts and chopped mint. Serve hot.

Serves 8.

Cajun Red Beans and Rice

This zesty bean and rice stew is easily made, but note that the beans must soak overnight. By omitting the ham or bacon, this recipe, as well as the variations, makes a superb vegetarian dish; adjust the seasoning accordingly. Serve with hot Skinny Corn Bread (page 152) and chilled beer.

1 pound dried red kidney beans, rinsed and sorted
2 large onions, chopped
1 green bell pepper, chopped
1 cup chopped celery
1 cup minced smoked turkey ham (about 1/4 pound)
1 teaspoon Cajun Pepper Mix (page 151)
1 1/2 cups long-grain brown rice
3 green onions, sliced thin, tops included
3 tablespoons minced parsley

Place the beans in a large heavy kettle, pour in 2 quarts boiling water, cover, and soak overnight.

Drain the beans well. Stir in 11 cups water, the onions, bell pepper, celery, ham, pepper mix, and rice. Bring to a boil over high heat, then reduce the heat to low, so that the liquid simmers. Cover and cook for 2 1/2 hours.

Stir in the green onions and parsley and cook, uncovered, on the lowest setting until most of the liquid is absorbed (about 30 minutes). Serve hot.

Serves 8.

Variations

Red Beans, Dominican Style. Substitute 2 cups small red beans (adzuki beans) for the kidney beans. Substitute 4 strips turkey bacon, fried, drained, and cut into pieces, for the ham. Omit the pepper mix and add 2 tomatoes, chopped; 1 teaspoon dried oregano; and 1/2 jalapeño pepper, minced. Cook for about 2 hours in all. Garnish with chopped cilantro.

Black Beans and Rice, Cuban Style. Substitute 1 pound dried black beans for the kidney beans. Substitute 2 slices turkey bacon, fried, drained, and cut into pieces, for the ham. Omit the pepper mix and add 2 large cloves garlic, minced; 1 small red chile, minced; 1 tablespoon red wine vinegar; 1/2 teaspoon dried cumin; and 1/8 teaspoon cayenne pepper. Cook for about 3 hours in all. Garnish with chopped cilantro rather than the parsley.

Feijoada

This unusual stew is considered the national dish of Brazil. Serve it with palm hearts and avocado slices on a bed of greens.

2 cups dried black beans, rinsed and sorted
1 cup long-grain brown rice
1/2 teaspoon salt
1 bay leaf
1 tablespoon olive oil
4 cups chopped onion
3 large cloves garlic, minced
1/2 pound smoked turkey sausage, cut into 1/2-inch pieces
1 pound tomatoes, chopped (about 2 cups)
1/4 teaspoon ground cumin
1/8 teaspoon crushed red pepper flakes
2 large oranges, peeled and chopped
1/4 cup chopped parsley
1 teaspoon grated orange zest
1/3 cup farina, toasted

Place the beans in a large Dutch oven. Cover with boiling water 2 inches above the beans and cook over high heat for 2 minutes. Remove from heat and let stand, covered, for 1 hour.

Drain the beans. Add 7 cups water, the rice, salt, and bay leaf. Bring to a boil, cover, reduce the heat, and simmer until the beans are tender (about 3 hours). Set aside but keep warm.

In a large skillet over medium-high heat, sauté the onion and garlic in the oil until tender (about 5 minutes). Add the sausage, tomatoes, cumin, and red pepper flakes and cook for 2 minutes.

Stir the tomato mixture into the reserved bean mixture and cook, uncovered, for 30 minutes. Top with the chopped oranges, parsley, and orange zest. Sprinkle with the toasted farina and serve.

Serves 8.

Three Grains and Ham

This variation on an Indian dish called *Keyma* takes some time to cook (note that the barley must soak overnight) but is very satisfying. Serve it with fresh green beans and sliced radishes on a bed of greens with Light Herb Dressing (page 149) and whole wheat bread.

1/2 cup hulled barley
2 tablespoons olive oil
2 ounces turkey ham, cut into 1/2-inch dice
3 large cloves garlic, sliced
1 large red onion, chopped
5 medium green onions, tops included, sliced
1/4 cup wild rice
4 cups Chicken Stock (page 146), divided
1 teaspoon dried oregano
1/2 cup lentils, rinsed
1/4 cup bulgur
1/4 cup firmly packed chopped parsley
Salt and freshly ground black pepper, to taste

Soak the barley in 2 1/2 cups water overnight.

In a large Dutch oven over medium heat, warm the oil. Sauté the ham, garlic, red onion, and green onions until soft (about 5 minutes). Add the rice, 2 cups of the stock, 1 cup water, and the oregano. Bring to a boil, then reduce the heat, cover, and simmer for 30 minutes.

Drain the barley and add it to the pot along with the lentils, bulgur, and remaining 2 cups stock. Cover and simmer until the grains are tender (about 40 minutes). Uncover and simmer until the liquid evaporates (about 10 minutes). Stir in the parsley. Add salt and freshly ground black pepper to taste. Serve immediately.

Serves 8.

Chicken Cacciatore

This chicken and vegetable combination is a popular Italian dish, best made with fresh tomatoes. Accompany it with steamed broccoli and young green beans, marinated, served at room temperature (see page 150), plus chunks of gusty Italian bread and dry white wine. Leftovers lend themselves to another delicious meal (see Note).

2 tablespoons olive oil
1 broiler-fryer chicken (about 3 pounds), cut into pieces
1/2 cup thinly sliced onion
2 cloves garlic, minced or pressed
1/2 pound fresh mushrooms, sliced thin
1 large green bell pepper, cut into strips
1 medium carrot, cut into very thin disks
4 cups chopped fresh Italian plum tomatoes or canned tomatoes, with juice
2 teaspoons Italian Herb Blend (page 150) *or* 1/2 teaspoon *each* dried basil, oregano, thyme, and marjoram
1/2 teaspoon salt
1/2 teaspoon freshly ground black pepper
1/2 cup Chicken Stock (page 146) or water
1/2 cup dry white wine
8 to 10 ounces whole wheat or semolina spaghetti
Parmesan cheese, for sprinkling (optional)

In a large skillet or Dutch oven with a lid, heat the oil over medium-high heat. Sauté the chicken pieces until golden brown. Set aside on a platter and sauté the onion and garlic until slightly browned.

Return the chicken to the pot and add the mushrooms, bell pepper, carrot, tomatoes, herb blend, salt, ground pepper, stock, and wine. Cover and simmer for about 1 hour. Remove the cover to let the sauce reduce somewhat and continue cooking until the chicken is very tender.

Cook the spaghetti according to directions on page 46. Drain and transfer to a serving bowl.

Remove the skin from the chicken pieces. Arrange the chicken over the hot spaghetti. Sprinkle with the Parmesan cheese, if desired. Serve at once.

Serves 4 to 6.

Note: If you have leftovers from this meal, remove the chicken from the bones and mince it. Add 2 inches mild Italian turkey sausage (cut into small pieces, fried, and drained) to the sauce and serve over freshly cooked spinach noodles or vegetable spirals.

Variation

Turkey Cacciatore. Substitute 4 cups cooked turkey (as much white meat as possible) for the chicken pieces. Cook about 1 hour in all.

Chicken Paprika

Adding mushrooms and peppers to the Austrian *Paprikahendl* is an adaptation of a recipe that comes from a Viennese friend. An elegant dish, it is traditionally served with noodles or steaming rice. Add a salad of soft head lettuce (Boston or buttercrunch) with Light Herb Dressing (page 149) and crisp dry white wine.

1 tablespoon light margarine
1 broiler-fryer chicken (about 3 pounds), cut into
    pieces
2 large onions, chopped
2 tablespoons sweet Hungarian paprika
1 tablespoon all-purpose flour
1/2 teaspoon salt
1/2 teaspoon freshly ground white pepper
1 can (8 ounces) whole tomatoes, chopped, with
    juice
1/4 pound fresh mushrooms, sliced
1/2 green bell pepper, sliced
1 pound egg noodles
1/2 cup buttermilk

In a large Dutch oven with a lid, heat the margarine over medium-high heat. Sauté the chicken pieces until slightly browned. Remove to a plate and set aside.

Reduce the heat to medium, add the onions, and sauté slowly until they are soft and golden. Stir in the paprika, flour, salt, ground pepper, and tomatoes. Stir well. Add the reserved chicken pieces, mushrooms, and bell pepper. Cover and simmer gently for about 45 minutes.

Cook the noodles in lightly salted water. Drain, then place on a heated platter. Arrange the chicken pieces on top and keep warm. Stir the buttermilk into the sauce and vegetables, heat thoroughly, and pour over the chicken. Serve immediately.

Serves 8.

Variation

Chicken Paprika with Dumplings. Omit the tomatoes and noodles. Add 1 cup Chicken Stock (page 146) with the chicken pieces. Cook the chicken for about 30 minutes; during that time prepare the dough for Parsley Dumplings (page 152). Stir the buttermilk into the sauce and bring to a boil. Drop the dumpling dough in 8 mounds on the simmering liquid. Reduce the heat, cover tightly, and cook for 20 minutes. Do not lift the lid to peek while the dumplings cook. Serve from the pot.

Brunswick Stew

From the American South, this dish in its original form contained no vegetables and was made from squirrel. The updated version given here changes both, although I am sorely tempted to try some of those squirrels that destroy my bird feeders. On second thought, let's stick to chicken. Serve this with a tossed green salad and Skinny Corn Bread (page 152).

1 tablespoon canola oil
All-purpose flour, salt, and freshly ground black pepper, for sprinkling
1 stewing chicken (about 4 pounds), cut into pieces
2 large onions, chopped
2 large cloves garlic, minced
2 large green bell peppers, chopped
1 cup chopped celery
2 tablespoons Worcestershire sauce, divided
1 tablespoon sweet Hungarian paprika
1 teaspoon dried thyme
1/4 cup finely chopped parsley
Generous dash red pepper flakes
8 cups peeled tomato or 1 can (28 ounces) whole tomatoes, with juice
2 packages (10 ounces each) frozen cut okra
2 packages (10 ounces each) frozen lima beans
3 cups corn kernels, cut from the cob, cooked

In a large Dutch oven with a lid, warm the oil over medium-high heat. Sprinkle the flour, salt, and ground pepper over the chicken pieces, then sauté until golden. Remove them to a platter and set aside.

Pour off any fat from the pot and add the onions, garlic, bell peppers, and celery. Cook, stirring, until the vegetables soften. Add 1 tablespoon of the Worcestershire sauce, the paprika, thyme, parsley, and pepper flakes; stir well.

Puree the tomato in the food processor. Add to the stew with the okra; mix well. Return the reserved chicken pieces to the pot, cover, and simmer for 1 hour, stirring occasionally. Add the lima beans and cook 30 minutes more, skimming off any scum that rises to the top.

Remove the chicken and set aside to cool slightly. Cut it up, discarding skin and bones, and return it to the pot. Stir in the corn and the remaining 1 tablespoon Worcestershire sauce; heat thoroughly before serving.

Serves 8 to 10.

Variation

Southern Chicken Stew with Carrot Dumplings. Omit the okra and add 1 cup Chicken Stock (page 146). After you have returned the cut-up chicken to the pot and added the corn, prepare the dough for Parsley Dumplings (page 152), adding 1/4 cup shredded carrot to the dough. Drop the dumplings onto the simmering liquid in 8 mounds. Cover tightly (don't peek) and cook for 15 minutes. Serves 8.

Arroz con Pollo

In international cuisine the chicken and rice combinations are almost limitless. This delicious Spanish dish, which has traveled to the Caribbean and South America, is one of the best known. Serve it with a green salad, chunks of hearty bread, and light, dry red wine.

2 tablespoons olive oil
Salt and freshly ground black pepper, to taste
1 broiler-fryer chicken (about 3 pounds), cut into pieces
2 cloves garlic, chopped
2 medium onions, chopped
4 ounces cooked turkey ham, diced
1 green bell pepper, chopped
1 red bell pepper, cut into strips
2 medium tomatoes, chopped
1 tablespoon paprika
1/4 teaspoon saffron threads, crushed in a mortar *or* 1/2 teaspoon ground saffron
2 1/4 cups long-grain brown rice
4 cups Chicken Stock (page 146)
1 package (10 ounces) frozen tiny peas
2 tablespoons finely chopped parsley, for garnish

In a heavy flameproof casserole over medium-high heat, warm the oil. Sprinkle the salt and pepper over the chicken pieces and sauté them until golden. Transfer to a plate and set aside. Then sauté the garlic, onions, ham, and bell peppers until the vegetables are soft. Add the tomatoes and cook until the mixture is thick (about 10 minutes).

Stir in the paprika and saffron, then add the rice and stock. Return the chicken pieces to the casserole. Taste and add more salt and ground pepper, if needed. Bring to a simmer, cover tightly, and cook over very low heat for 30 minutes. Stir in the peas and continue to cook, covered, until the chicken is tender and almost all the liquid has been absorbed. Don't worry if the dish seems somewhat soupy.

Remove it from the heat and let it stand, covered, for 10 minutes; the remaining liquid will be absorbed. Garnish with the parsley and serve hot.

Serves 6.

Variation

Chicken and Rice, Moroccan Style. Omit the ham and tomatoes. Sauté 1/2 cup slivered almonds, 1/2 teaspoon ground ginger, and 1/8 teaspoon tumeric with the vegetables. Reduce the paprika to 1 teaspoon. Stir in 2 cups cooked chick-peas and 3 tablespoons lemon juice with the peas.

Chicken and Rice, Arabian Style

This chicken and rice combination, called *Kabsa*, is one of Saudi Arabia's favorite dishes and a fine illustration of the interesting flavors of this region. Serve it with a salad of thinly sliced zucchini and cucumber topped with Creamy Vinaigrette (page 149) and warm whole wheat pita bread.

2 cups long-grain white rice
2 tablespoons canola oil
2 medium onions, sliced
5 cloves garlic, crushed
1 broiler-fryer chicken (about 3 pounds), cut into pieces, all fat and skin removed
1/2 cup Tomato Puree (page 148)
2 medium tomatoes, chopped
3 cups hot water
2 medium carrots, grated
Grated zest of 1 orange
6 whole cloves
6 whole cardamom seeds
4 sticks cinnamon
1/2 teaspoon salt
1/2 teaspoon freshly ground white pepper
1/4 cup raisins
1/4 cup almonds, blanched and sliced

Cover the rice with boiling water and soak for at least 15 minutes.

In a large Dutch oven with a lid, warm the oil over medium heat. Sauté the onions and garlic until they begin to brown. Add the chicken pieces, tomato puree, and chopped tomatoes and cook over low heat, stirring, for about 5 minutes. Add the hot water, grated carrots, orange zest, cloves, cardamom, cinnamon, salt, and ground pepper. Cook over low heat for 20 to 25 minutes. Remove the chicken and keep warm.

Drain the rice and add it to the sauce. Continue cooking the sauce slowly until the rice is cooked and dry (about 15 minutes). Transfer the rice to a heated platter, arrange the reserved chicken pieces on top, and garnish with the raisins and almonds. Serve immediately.

Serves 8.

Paella

This colorful medley of meats, seafood, vegetables, and rice is Spain's most popular dish and makes superb party fare. Despite the varied ingredients, once everything is assembled the dish is quickly made. If you don't have a paella pan, use a 16-inch skillet or large sauté pan with a lid, or a flameproof casserole. Serve this dish with hearty whole wheat bread and light red wine.

3 pounds chicken breasts, split
Salt and freshly ground pepper, to taste
2 tablespoons olive oil
4 ounces lean pork tenderloin, chopped
4 ounces garlic-flavored turkey sausage, cut into
  1/4-inch slices
4 ounces turkey ham, chopped
2 medium onions, chopped fine
4 cloves garlic, chopped
2 red bell peppers, sliced
12 large shrimp, shelled (tails left on) and deveined
1 lobster tail, cut into 8 pieces
3 cups short-grain white rice
3 tablespoons chopped parsley
1 bay leaf
1/4 teaspoon saffron threads, crushed in a mortar, *or* 1 teaspoon ground saffron
6 cups Chicken Stock (page 146)
1 cup fresh peas *or* 1 package (10 ounces) frozen
  peas, defrosted
16 clams, scrubbed
16 mussels, scrubbed
Lemon wedges, for garnish
Chopped parsley, for garnish

Season the chicken pieces with the salt and ground pepper. In a paella pan over medium-high heat, warm the oil. Sauté the chicken until golden. Transfer to a platter and keep warm.

Add the pork, sausage, and ham to the pan and cook, stirring, for about 10 minutes. Transfer to a plate and set aside. Reduce the heat to medium and add the onions, garlic, and bell peppers; sauté until the onions are soft. Add the shrimp and lobster pieces and cook just until they turn pink (no more than 3 minutes). Transfer to a plate and set aside.

Return the pork combination to the pan, then stir in the rice, parsley, bay leaf, and saffron. Pour in the stock, stir to mix, and cook, uncovered, stirring from time to time, for 10 minutes. Stir in the peas. Bury the reserved chicken pieces in the rice together with the reserved seafood. Push the clams and mussels into the rice, with the side that will open uppermost, if possible. Cover tightly and cook over the lowest heat until the rice is tender and all the liquid is absorbed.

Let stand, covered, for 10 minutes. Serve directly from the paella pan, garnished with the lemon wedges and sprinkled with the chopped parsley.

Serves 8.

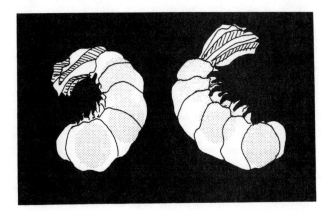

Turkey and Bacon Stew

This northeastern American stew offers a good way to use up leftover turkey from the holidays. Use as much white meat as possible and enjoy the savory blend of turkey, vegetables, and herbs. Serve it with Triple Wheat Biscuits (page 152) or Skinny Corn Bread (page 152) and a mixed green salad with Creamy Vinaigrette (page 149).

2 slices turkey bacon, diced
2 large onions, chopped
2 carrots, sliced thin
4 ribs celery, sliced in thin diagonals
1/4 pound mushrooms, sliced
2 tablespoons all-purpose flour
1 tablespoon wheat germ
4 medium red potatoes, unpeeled and diced
1 teaspoon dried thyme
1/2 teaspoon rubbed dried sage
2 bay leaves
1/2 teaspoon salt
1/2 teaspoon freshly ground white pepper
2 cups Turkey Stock (page 146) *or* Chicken Stock
   (page 146)
1/2 cup dry white wine or dry sherry
2 cups diced cooked turkey
1/2 cup plain nonfat yogurt
Chopped parsley, for garnish

In a large stove-top casserole over medium heat, fry the bacon until crisp. Drain on paper towels. Drain off most of the fat. Sauté the onions, carrots, and celery until soft; then stir in the mushrooms and cook for 2 minutes. Add the flour and wheat germ and cook for 2 minutes longer. Stir in the potatoes.

Remove the casserole from the heat and add the thyme, sage, bay leaves, salt, ground pepper, stock, and wine. Stir well. Cook over low heat for 45 minutes. Add the turkey and reserved bacon and cook for 15 minutes. Stir in the yogurt and heat thoroughly but do not boil.

Remove from the heat, discard the bay leaves, and sprinkle each portion with the parsley. Serve hot.

Serves 6.

Salmon Jambalaya

This adaptation of a traditional Cajun dish nicely illustrates the lively flavors of Louisiana cooking. Serve it with a salad of romaine, shredded spinach, and sweet head lettuce topped with Light Herb Dressing (page 149), and chilled dry white wine.

1 tablespoon light margarine
1 cup chopped onion
1 cup sliced celery
1 cup coarsely chopped green bell pepper
2 cloves garlic, crushed in a garlic press
1 cup diced turkey ham
1 1/2 cups long-grain white rice
1/2 teaspoon dried thyme
1/2 teaspoon Cajun Pepper Mix (page 151)
1/4 teaspoon salt
1/4 teaspoon freshly ground white pepper
2 cups coarsely chopped tomato
3 cups Chicken Stock (page 146)
Water, if needed
1 1/2 cups flaked cooked fresh salmon

In a large skillet with a lid, melt the margarine over medium heat. Sauté the onion, celery, bell pepper, and garlic until the onion is soft. Add the ham, rice, thyme, pepper mix, salt, and ground pepper. Cook, stirring, for a 10 minutes. Add the chopped tomato and stock; bring to a boil and cook, uncovered, for 5 minutes.

Reduce the heat to low, cover, and simmer for 45 to 50 minutes, stirring occasionally. Add a little water if the jambalaya seems to be getting too dry. Add the salmon and cook until heated through (about 5 minutes). Serve at once.

Serves 6.

Mediterranean Trout Stew

This simple combination of fish and rice makes an easy and delicate supper dish. Serve it with crusty whole-grain bread to soak up the juices.

1 tablespoon olive oil
1 cup long-grain brown rice
1 cup chopped celery
1 cup chopped onion
1/2 cup minced watercress or chopped green bell pepper
3 cloves garlic, minced
1/2 teaspoon sweet Hungarian paprika
1/2 teaspoon dried thyme
2 cups Fish Stock (page 146)
1 pound trout fillets
1 cup chopped peeled Italian plum tomatoes
1 package (10 ounces) frozen tiny peas, defrosted

In a stove-top casserole over medium heat, warm the oil. Sauté the rice, celery, onion, watercress, garlic, paprika, and thyme, stirring constantly, until the mixture is fragrant (3 to 4 minutes).

Add the stock, increase the heat to high, and bring to a boil. Reduce the heat to low, cover, and simmer until the rice is almost cooked (about 40 minutes). Add the fish, cover, and simmer for 10 minutes. Stir in the tomatoes and peas, cover, and simmer until completely heated through. Serve hot.

Serves 4.

Variation

Monkfish, Mediterranean Style. Instead of the trout, use 1 pound monkfish fillets, skinned and cut into 1-inch slices. Substitute 2 red bell peppers, cut into strips, for the watercress. Garnish with lemon slices.

Southwest Seafood Stew

This hearty and nourishing stew combines the strong, hot flavors of the American Southwest with the colors and textures of fresh vegetables, legumes, and different kinds of seafood. It is easily made. Serve it with Skinny Corn Bread (page 152) or toasted corn tortillas, and chilled beer.

2 tablespoons olive oil, divided
2 medium zucchini, cut in half lengthwise, then sliced
2 medium onions, chopped coarsely
4 cloves garlic, minced
1 large red bell pepper, diced
1 large yellow or green bell pepper, diced
1 small jalapeño pepper, seeded and diced
1 can (28 ounces) plum tomatoes, chopped, with juice
5 medium fresh tomatoes, chopped coarsely
1/2 pound fresh mushrooms, sliced
1 tablespoon dried basil
1 tablespoon dried oregano
1 tablespoon chili powder
2 teaspoons ground cumin
1 teaspoon freshly ground black pepper
1 teaspoon fennel seeds
1/2 cup chopped cilantro or flat-leaf (Italian) parsley
1 cup cooked kidney beans, drained
1 cup cooked chick-peas, drained
1 pound cooked seafood mixture, such as medium shrimp, crabmeat, scallops, tuna, and lobster tail
2 tablespoons fresh lemon juice
4 cups hot cooked long-grain white rice
Shredded reduced-fat Monterey jack cheese, for garnish

In a large heavy Dutch oven over medium heat, warm 1 tablespoon of the oil. Sauté the zucchini until just tender. With a slotted spoon remove it to a plate and set aside.

Add the remaining 1 tablespoon oil to the pot. Sauté the onions, garlic, bell peppers, and jalapeño pepper until tender (about 8 minutes).

Reduce the heat to low and stir in the reserved zucchini, the canned and fresh tomatoes, mushrooms, basil, oregano, chili powder, cumin, ground pepper, fennel seeds, and cilantro. Cook, uncovered and stirring often, for 30 minutes. Stir in the beans and chick-peas and cook for 10 minutes more. Add the seafood mixture and cook until it is heated through. Stir in the lemon juice.

Serve the stew over the rice and sprinkle the shredded cheese over each portion.

Serves 8.

Fisherman's Stew, Portuguese Style

This dish, called *Caldeirada a pescadora* in Portugal, is a delicious stew with very simple ingredients. Serve it from the casserole with crusty bread and dry white wine.

1 tablespoon olive oil
4 onions, sliced
3 large cloves garlic, minced
1 green bell pepper, chopped
1 red bell pepper, chopped
1/4 cup chopped parsley
1 teaspoon coriander seeds
2 pounds mixed fish, such as haddock, cod, or sea bass, cut into bite-sized pieces
5 medium tomatoes, peeled and chopped, *or* 2 cups chopped canned tomatoes, with juice
6 medium potatoes, halved, then sliced
1 bay leaf
1/2 teaspoon salt
1/2 teaspoon freshly ground white pepper
1 cup dry white wine

In a deep stove-top casserole with a lid, warm the oil over medium heat. Sauté the onions, garlic, bell pepper, parsley, and coriander seeds until the onions are golden. Stir in the fish, tomatoes, potatoes, bay leaf, salt, ground pepper, and wine. Add just enough water to cover. Cover the casserole and simmer for about 45 minutes. Remove from the heat, discard the bay leaf, and serve at once.

Serves 6 to 8.

Variation

Mussel Stew, Mediterranean Style. Sauté 1/4 pound sliced fresh mushrooms with the onions and garlic. Substitute 4 pounds mussels, well scrubbed and debearded, for the fish; add them after the stew has cooked for about 30 minutes.

Rishtayeh

This Syrian dish is an unusual yet simple combination of ingredients. An interesting accompaniment would be tomatoes stuffed with rice, currants, pine nuts, and chopped mint, then baked.

1 cup lentils, rinsed
6 cups water
1 tablespoon olive oil
2 medium onions, sliced
1 large clove garlic, minced
1 cup minced parsley
1 package (10 ounces) fresh spinach, stems removed, leaves chopped, *or* 1 package (10 ounces) frozen chopped spinach
2 cups flat noodles, spirals, or elbow macaroni
Salt, to taste

In a large stove-top casserole, combine the lentils and the water. Bring to a boil, then simmer until the lentils are tender (45 to 60 minutes).

In a medium skillet over medium heat, warm the oil. Sauté the onions, garlic, and parsley until the onions are soft. Add to the cooked lentils.

Stir the spinach and noodles into the casserole. Taste and add the salt, if necessary. Let simmer until the noodles are cooked (about 10 minutes), adding water if necessary. Serve hot.

Serves 8.

Lentils, Monastery Style

An adaptation of a popular Spanish soup, this dish is an all-time favorite in my house. It is simple, unusual, and delicious. Serve it with a mixed green salad or slightly cooked, marinated vegetables, such as green beans, broccoli, and bell peppers. Chilled beer or dry white wine go well with the dish. Don't forget chunks of hearty bread to soak up the juices.

2 tablespoons olive oil
2 large onions, chopped
2 large carrots, chopped or sliced thin
2 medium potatoes, cut into 1-inch cubes
1 teaspoon dried thyme
1/2 teaspoon dried marjoram
3 cups Vegetable Stock (page 147)
1 cup lentils, rinsed
1/4 cup chopped parsley
1 can (28 ounces) tomatoes, chopped, with juice
1/2 teaspoon salt, or to taste
1/4 cup dry sherry (optional)
2 tablespoons shredded reduced-fat sharp Cheddar cheese

In a stove-top casserole over medium heat, warm the oil. Sauté the onions, carrots, and potatoes for about 5 minutes. Add the thyme and marjoram and sauté for 1 minute longer.

Reduce the heat to low and stir in the stock, lentils, parsley, and tomatoes. Add the salt and cook, covered, for about 45 minutes. Stir in the sherry, if desired.

To serve, sprinkle the cheese on top of each portion.

Serves 4 to 6.

Variations

Lentil-eggplant Stew, Sicilian Style. Sauté 3 cloves garlic, minced, with the other vegetables. With the addition of the stock and other ingredients, stir in 1 small eggplant, peeled and cut into 1/2-inch cubes, and 1/4 cup dry red wine. Omit the sherry. Cook as above. Serves 6.

Lentils and Rice. For this variation of a Middle Eastern dish called *Mujaddara*, omit the potatoes, tomatoes, sherry, and cheese. Add 5 cups water and 3/4 cup long-grain brown rice. Simmer until the rice is tender. Taste and adjust the seasoning, then simmer, uncovered, until the liquid is absorbed. The *Mujaddara* is usually cooked ahead of time and eaten at room temperature.

Moroccan Spicy Vegetable Stew

For an authentic rendition of this recipe, you should prepare the couscous as indicated below, allowing about 1 hour cooking time. Yes, you can buy it in a box, and it cooks up very quickly, but it can be tasteless and gluey. If possible, buy the couscous in bulk at the natural foods store and enjoy the savory smells of this dish as everything cooks slowly. Serve this stew with chunks of hearty whole wheat bread and a lightly minted tea.

1 cup couscous
3 tablespoons olive oil, divided
1/2 cup cold water
1 large onion, chopped
1 large green bell pepper, chopped
1 large red bell pepper, chopped
2 carrots, sliced thin
1 cup chopped tomato *or* 1 can (8 ounces) whole
   tomatoes, chopped, with juice
1 cup Vegetable Stock (page 147)
1 tablespoon lemon juice
1 teaspoon ground coriander
1/2 teaspoon ground cinnamon
1/2 teaspoon saffron threads, crushed, *or* 1/4
   teaspoon ground saffron
3/4 teaspoon salt, divided
2 cups cooked chick-peas, drained, *or* 1 can (15
   ounces) chick-peas, rinsed and drained
1 medium zucchini, quartered lengthwise, then
   sliced
1/2 cup hot water
Toasted sesame seeds, for garnish
Hot Pepper Sauce (page 148; see Note)

To prepare the couscous, combine it with 1 tablespoon of the oil, stir well, and pour into the steam pan of a couscousière or a shallow colander that fits inside a stove-top casserole or Dutch oven with a tight-fitting lid. If the holes in the colander are too large, line it with dampened cheesecloth. Steam the couscous over simmering water or stock for 20 minutes. Transfer the couscous to a bowl and stir in 1/2 cup cold water, breaking up all the lumps with a fork. Return the couscous to the steam pan or colander.

Meanwhile, in a large stove-top casserole or Dutch oven with a tight-fitting lid, warm the remaining 2 tablespoons oil. Sauté the onion over medium heat until softened; then add the bell peppers and carrots and cook for 5 minutes. Stir in the tomato, stock, lemon juice, coriander, cinnamon, saffron, and 1/2 teaspoon of the salt. Mix well.

Place the couscous container on top of the casserole, cover, and simmer for 15 minutes. Uncover. Stir the chick-peas and zucchini into the vegetable mixture. Return the couscous to a bowl and stir in the remaining 1/4 teaspoon salt and the 1/2 cup hot water. Return the couscous mixture to the steam pan, replace the pan over the vegetable mixture, cover, and simmer for 10 to 15 minutes.

Fluff up the couscous with a fork. Spoon it around the edge of a large, deep platter and arrange the vegetables in the center. Sprinkle the sesame seeds over the top.

Pass the Hot Pepper Sauce.

Serves 6.

Note: If you prefer, omit the Hot Pepper Sauce and add 1/4 teaspoon ground cumin and 1/4 teaspoon red pepper flakes with the coriander and cinnamon.

Vegetarian Chili

This wonderful dish takes a while to cook, but it is hearty and delicious. Serve it with a salad of romaine and orange slices and Creamy Orange Dressing (page 150), and lots of Skinny Corn Bread (page 152).

2 1/2 cups dried kidney beans
6 cups boiling water
1 teaspoon salt, divided
1 cup medium-grain bulgur
1 cup tomato juice
1 tablespoon canola oil
3 medium onions, chopped
4 cloves garlic, minced
1 cup chopped celery
1 cup chopped carrot
1 cup chopped green bell pepper
2 teaspoons minced jalapeño pepper
2 teaspoons chili powder
Juice of 1/2 lemon
1 teaspoon ground cumin
1 teaspoon dried basil
2 cups chopped tomato
1/4 cup dry red wine
Dash cayenne pepper
1/4 cup chopped cilantro or parsley
1/2 cup plain nonfat yogurt

Place the kidney beans in a large pot, cover with the boiling water, and soak for 6 hours. Drain, cover with fresh water and 1/2 teaspoon of the salt, and cook until tender (about 1 hour), adding more water if needed.

Measure the bulgur into a medium bowl. Bring the tomato juice to a boil and pour over the bulgur. Let stand.

In a large stove-top casserole or Dutch oven over medium heat, warm the oil. Sauté the onions and garlic until softened; reduce the heat to medium-low, stir in the celery and carrot, and cook for about 10 minutes. Add the bell pepper, jalapeño pepper, chili powder, lemon juice, cumin, basil, and the remaining 1/2 teaspoon salt; cook until the peppers are tender.

Reduce the heat to low, stir in the tomato, reserved bulgur, cooked beans, wine, and cayenne. Combine well and simmer for about 30 minutes. Top with the chopped cilantro and serve the yogurt on the side.

Serves 4 to 6.

Variation

Quick Vegetarian Chili. Substitute 2 cans (15 ounces each) red kidney beans, drained and rinsed, for the uncooked beans. Substitute 1 can (28 ounces) whole tomatoes, chopped, with juice, for the fresh tomato. Omit the wine. Prepare the bulgur and sautéed vegetables as above; then combine the other ingredients and simmer, uncovered, for 15 to 20 minutes.

Meals from
the Soup Pot

No matter the time of year, soup is good, nutritious food. A bowl of steaming soup provides comfort for both body and soul.

There are few culinary endeavors easier than making soup. It is close to impossible to ruin a pot of soup, short of burning the bottom of the pan or adding too much salt.

When making soup, exact quantities are not terribly important and interesting combinations are often desirable. It is reassuring to know that a combination of various foods, cooked in water and/or stock, and judiciously seasoned, can be virtually a foolproof creation.

Soup is more often than not made from economical ingredients, frequently leftovers from the refrigerator or staples found on the pantry shelf. The best soup, although it may simmer a long time, is made fresh. There is no harm, though, in keeping a container in the refrigerator for several days into which you add leftover foods and the stock from vegetables, which can serve as the basis for a delicious soup. I keep just such a container in the freezer. When I am ready to make soup, I just defrost it and add it to the pot.

The success of a good soup often depends on a good stock to start with. Canned broth, and especially commercial broth cubes and powders meant to be dissolved in water, can contain unacceptable amounts of additives (salt, for example), so I do not recommend them. The best bet—both nutritionally and economically—is to make the stock yourself Recipes for basic soup stocks are in the Appendix, and the soups this book refer to them. But you can use whatever stock you have on hand, provided you keep within the same general range of ingredients.

The recipes presented here are for hearty soups, those that provide a complete meal. This kind of soup seems for the most part a North American concept. In general, and especially in European cuisines, soups are served as a first course and are not considered sufficient for the main dish. For this reason, the suggestions made for accompaniments are my own rather than from a particular ethnic tradition.

I always look forward to a good bowl of soup. Remember that in general the longer the soup simmers, the more flavorful it becomes. So allow time for the cooking and enjoy the gathering of family and friends around the soup tureen.

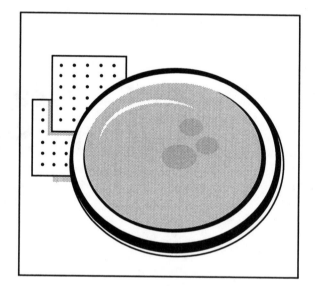

Pot au Feu

This soup is the French equivalent of a New England boiled dinner. If you were to eat it in France, the broth would be served as the first course; it would be followed by the meat and vegetables as the main course, with plenty of *gros sel* (sea salt) and Dijon mustard. This is a hearty main dish. Serve it with thickly sliced whole wheat bread and hearty red wine.

**1 pound beef shinbone, preferably cut into 2
  pieces, all visible fat removed**
1/2 teaspoon salt
6 cups cold water
6 leeks
2 large onions, chopped
3 carrots, sliced thin
3 celery stalks, with tops, chopped
2 parsnips, cubed (optional)
3 medium potatoes, cut into 1-inch cubes
4 black peppercorns
1 bay leaf
1 tablespoon chopped parsley
1 teaspoon dried thyme

Place the shinbone in a soup pot or large saucepan. Sprinkle with the salt and let stand for 1 hour.

Add the cold water and let stand for 30 minutes. Cover and bring to a boil over high heat, then reduce the heat and simmer for 3 hours. Skim, if desired.

Add the leeks, onions, carrots, celery, parsnips (if desired), potatoes, peppercorns, bay leaf, parsley, and thyme (see Note). Simmer the soup until the vegetables are done (about 40 minutes).

Taste and adjust the seasoning, if necessary. Strain off 2 or more cups of the broth for other use. Remove the meat from the bones and trim away any fat, then cut the meat into very small pieces and return to the soup. Serve hot.

Serves 4 to 6.

Note: Alternatively, make a cheesecloth bag and put in it 6 parsley sprigs, 2 sprigs fresh thyme, 1 bay leaf, 4 peppercorns, and 4 cloves garlic.

Variation
Beef and Barley Soup. When boiling the beef, stir in 1/2 cup hulled barley and use only 1 potato. Omit the parsnips; add 2 cups cut green beans, fresh or frozen, and 1 can (28 ounces) whole tomatoes, chopped, with juice, along with the vegetables. Serves 6.

Korean Hot Beef Soup

This doubly hot soup has typical Korean fiery flavors provided by the ginger, chile pepper, and mustard. Accompany it with a chilled spinach salad with Sesame Dressing (page 150).

3 ounces flank steak, trimmed of all visible fat
   and frozen for 30 minutes
2 cloves garlic, minced
2 teaspoons low-sodium soy sauce
1 teaspoon minced peeled fresh ginger
1 teaspoon dry mustard
1 teaspoon sesame oil
3 cups Beef Stock (page 146)
2 tablespoons rice vinegar
2 cups shredded Chinese cabbage
1 large green bell pepper, cut into small strips
10 green onions, sliced thin
1/4 pound small mushrooms, cut into quarters
Part of a dried Asian chile, crumbled, to taste
8 ounces firm tofu, cubed
3 cups hot cooked short-grain white rice

Cut the briefly frozen beef across the grain into paper-thin slices, then into 1-inch lengths.

In a wide, shallow bowl, combine the garlic, soy sauce, fresh ginger, mustard, and sesame oil. Add the beef slices and toss to coat. Set aside.

In a large soup pot, combine the stock, vinegar, cabbage, bell pepper, green onions, mushrooms, and crumbled chile. Bring to a boil, then reduce the heat and simmer, covered, for about 10 minutes.

In a large nonstick skillet over medium-high heat, sear the reserved beef until no longer pink (about 3 minutes). Add to the soup. Spoon about 1/4 cup of the soup liquid into the pan to deglaze it, stir well, then return the liquid to the soup along with the tofu. Cook for 5 minutes to heat through.

Divide the rice among 6 soup bowls. Pour in the soup and serve at once.

Serves 6.

Ukrainian Borscht

There are many varieties of borscht, all characteristically hearty and filled with different vegetables. Serve this with thick slices of Russian pumpernickel bread.

1 tablespoon canola oil
1 pound lean top round, all visible fat removed,
   cut into 1-inch cubes
3 cups Beef Stock (page 146)
2 cups water
4 cups shredded cabbage
2 cups shredded beet
2 medium tomatoes, peeled and chopped
1 cup sliced carrot
1 cup chopped onion
2 teaspoons sugar
1 1/2 teaspoons cider vinegar
2 large potatoes, cubed
1/4 cup Tomato Puree (page 148) *or* 2 tablespoons
   Crushed Tomatoes (page 148) *or* tomato paste
1 tablespoon chopped parsley
1 tablespoon dried dill weed
1/2 teaspoon salt
1/2 teaspoon freshly ground black pepper
1 cup plain low-fat yogurt

In a large saucepan or soup pot over medium-high heat, warm the oil. Add the meat, in batches, and sear on all sides. Drain the fat from the pan and pour in the stock and water. Add the cabbage, beet, tomatoes, carrot, onion, sugar, and vinegar. Bring to a boil; then reduce the heat, cover, and simmer for about 1 hour.

Stir in the potatoes, Tomato Puree, parsley, dill, salt, and ground pepper. Cover and simmer until the potatoes are tender (about 30 minutes). Ladle the borscht into soup bowls and top each portion with 2 tablespoons of the yogurt. Serve hot.

Serves 6 to 8.

Mexican-style Meatball Soup

This dish has many of the same ingredients as chili, but with added vegetables, tasty meatballs, and a rich broth. Serve it with Skinny Corn Bread (page 152), a mixed green salad, and chilled beer.

3/4 pound lean ground beef
4 teaspoons chopped canned green chiles
2 tablespoons chopped parsley
1 large clove garlic, pressed
1/2 teaspoon ground cumin
1/4 teaspoon salt
3 tablespoons cornmeal
1 1/4 cups Beef Stock (page 146), divided
1 cup water
1 can (28 ounces) whole tomatoes, chopped, with juice
3 medium potatoes, diced
1 can (20 ounces) red kidney beans, undrained
1 cup fresh or frozen corn kernels
2 stalks celery, chopped
1/2 teaspoon chili powder
1/4 teaspoon cayenne pepper
4 green onions, with tops, sliced thin

In a large bowl lightly mix the beef, chiles, parsley, garlic, cumin, salt, cornmeal, and 3 table-spoons of the stock. Shape into 16 meatballs; set aside.

In a large saucepan or soup pot, combine the remaining stock with the water, tomatoes, potatoes, beans, corn, celery, chili powder, and cayenne. Bring to a boil and add the reserved meatballs, then reduce the heat, cover, and simmer for about 30 minutes. Garnish with the green onions and serve.

Serves 8.

Scotch Broth

This is a classic soup, one I remember from my childhood. You can make it with leftover roast leg of lamb, or with stewing lamb (ask your butcher to give you the bones). Serve it with a green salad and Triple Wheat Biscuits (page 152).

1 cup hulled barley
2 cups lamb pieces from a roast, all visible fat removed, plus the bone, *or* 1 pound stewing lamb, all visible fat removed
4 cups water, or more as needed
4 cups Root Vegetable Stock (page 147)
1/2 teaspoon salt, or more to taste
1/2 teaspoon freshly ground black pepper
1 cup (about half the 10-ounce package) frozen butter beans
1 tablespoon canola oil
3 carrots, cut into small chunks
2 stalks celery, with tops, chopped
2 small potatoes, cubed
2 medium onions, chopped
2 cloves garlic, minced
1/4 cup chopped parsley, for garnish

Soak the barley in water for 2 hours. Drain.

In a Dutch oven over medium-high heat, brown the meat and bones. Drain off any fat, pour in the water and stock, and bring to a boil. Add the drained barley, salt, and ground pepper. Cover and simmer until the meat is tender and the barley is cooked (about 2 hours). Remove the bones. Stir in the beans.

In a nonstick skillet over medium heat, warm the oil. Add the carrots, celery, potatoes, onions, and garlic. Sauté for about 5 minutes; then add the vege-tables to the soup and cook until they are tender (20 to 30 minutes), adding more water if necessary. Just before serving, taste and add more salt if desired. Garnish with the parsley and serve.

Serves 8.

Winter Beef and Vegetable Soup

Serve this tasty soup with thick slices of whole wheat bread.

1 tablespoon canola oil
3 onions, chopped
1 pound lean ground beef
2 large cloves garlic, minced
3 cups Beef Stock (page 146)
2 cans (28 ounces each) tomatoes, chopped, with juice
1 cup diced potato
1 cup chopped celery
1 cup fresh or frozen cut green beans
2 carrots, chopped
1/4 cup brown rice or pearl barley
1 cup dry red wine
2 tablespoons chopped parsley
1 teaspoon dried basil
1/2 teaspoon dried thyme
1/2 teaspoon salt
1/2 teaspoon freshly ground black pepper

In a large soup pot over medium heat, warm the oil. Sauté the onions until they are soft and lightly browned. Stir in the beef and garlic and cook, separating the beef with a fork, until it is brown. Drain off any excess fat.

Add the remaining ingredients, cover, and bring to a boil. Reduce the heat and simmer for about 1 hour, adding 1/2 cup water, if needed. Taste and adjust the seasoning before serving.

Serves 8 to 10.

Variations

Hungarian Goulash Soup. Omit the green beans, carrots, and rice (or barley); increase the diced potato to 2 cups. Instead of parsley, basil, and thyme, substitute 1 teaspoon paprika (preferably hot), 1/4 teaspoon cayenne pepper, and 1/4 teaspoon caraway seeds. Serves 8.

Winter Beef Soup, Spanish Style. Omit the green beans and add 1 cup sliced summer squash and 1 cup cooked chick-peas. Use 1/2 cup brown rice.

Boerenkass Soup

The name of this delicious concoction from the Netherlands means "cheese soup of the farmers." If you can't find Gouda in a reduced-fat form, use a cheese slicer and make very thin slices, or substitute reduced-fat Jarlsberg, which works well. This soup is good with chilled beer.

2 teaspoons light margarine
1 medium onion, chopped
2 cups cauliflower florets
2 medium potatoes, diced
1/2 cup chopped carrot
1/2 cup chopped celeriac or chopped celery stalks, tops, and root
2 cups water
2 cups Chicken Stock (page 146)
1/2 teaspoon freshly ground white pepper
1/4 teaspoon sweet Hungarian paprika
Vegetable spray, for skillet
2 ounces Canadian-style bacon, cut into pieces, *or* 1/4 cup diced cooked ham
4 thin slices French bread, lightly toasted
4 thin slices reduced-fat Gouda or Jarlsberg cheese

In a 4-quart saucepan or soup pot over medium heat, warm the margarine until it is bubbly. Add the onion and sauté until soft. Stir in the cauliflower, potatoes, carrot, and celeriac; sauté for 5 minutes. Add the water, stock, ground pepper, and paprika; stir to combine. Bring to a boil; then reduce the heat to low, cover, and let simmer until the vegetables are just tender (about 15 minutes).

Spray a small nonstick skillet with vegetable spray. Add the bacon and brown lightly. If using ham, omit this step. Stir it into the soup and heat thoroughly.

Pour the soup into 4 flameproof crocks or bowls. Top each portion with a slice of toasted bread and a slice of cheese. Place under the broiler until the cheese is bubbly (about 4 minutes), watching carefully so that it doesn't burn.

Serves 4.

Ham and Potato Chowder

The term chowder has a rather mysterious etymological history.

The first chowders were made of fish and appeared in New England in the early eighteenth century. The term has come to refer most often to milk-based soups containing clams, although there is a substantial regional difference between New York clam chowder, which adds tomatoes, and the New England version, which would never. Today the term seems more general, referring to a milk-based soup, with or without fish, with or without meat, but always with potatoes. Serve this chowder with a salad of greens and fresh sliced tomatoes, and hearty dark rye bread.

1 tablespoon light margarine
1 cup chopped onion
1/2 cup chopped green bell pepper
1/2 cup chopped celery
1/2 cup chopped carrot
4 medium russet potatoes, diced
2 1/3 cups water, divided
1/4 teaspoon freshly ground white pepper
1/4 teaspoon mild paprika
2 tablespoons all-purpose flour
2 cups skim milk
1 package (10 ounces) frozen corn kernels, defrosted
3/4 cup finely chopped smoked ham or turkey ham
2 tablespoons minced parsley, for garnish
2 tablespoons shredded reduced-fat Cheddar cheese (optional)

In a large saucepan or soup pot over medium heat, melt the margarine. Sauté the onion, bell pepper, celery, and carrot until tender. Add the potatoes, 2 cups of the water, the ground pepper, and paprika. Cover and simmer until the potatoes are tender.

Make a paste of the flour and the remaining 1/3 cup water. Spoon some of the hot broth into the paste and stir well to blend, then add it to the soup along with the milk. Cook, stirring constantly, until slightly thickened. Stir in the corn and ham. Heat thoroughly.

To serve, ladle into bowls and garnish with the chopped parsley and cheese, if desired.

Serves 6 generously.

Variations

Potato and Sausage Chowder. Substitute about 5 ounces bulk turkey sausage for the ham. Shape it into very small balls and fry it in a small skillet until well browned. Drain off the fat and stir the sausage in with the corn. Garnish with 1/4 cup cheese.

Chicken and Corn Chowder. Substitute 3/4 cup minced cooked chicken for the ham. Substitute 2 cups Chicken Stock (page 146) for 2 cups of the water. If desired, add 1 teaspoon curry powder when sautéing the vegetables.

Caldo Verde

This soup from Portugal is one of the country's most popular. The green color of the soup is from Galician cabbage, which has large deep green leaves and is more like kale than cabbage. The greens are cut to an almost grasslike fineness, a task made easier by rolling them into a tube before slicing. With this soup the Portuguese would eat a chewy bread, such as *broa*, a delicious yeast corn bread. Instead you could substitute thick slices of whole wheat or rye bread. Serve this soup with light dry white wine.

1/2 pound fresh kale or collard greens
4 ounces smoked turkey sausage (kielbasa is the closest substitute for Portuguese sausage)
2 tablespoons olive oil
1 medium onion, chopped fine
3 medium potatoes (about 1 pound), peeled and sliced thin
6 cups water
1/2 teaspoon salt
1/4 teaspoon freshly ground black pepper

Wash the greens under cold running water. Trim bruised or blemished spots and cut away the coarse stems and veins. Stack the leaves, about 6 at a time, then roll up and slice very thin with a sharp knife. Set aside.

In a small nonstick skillet over medium heat, sauté the sausage until lightly browned. Drain on paper towels, slice into 1/4-inch-thick rounds, and set aside.

In a large saucepan or soup pot over medium heat, warm the oil. Sauté the onion until soft. Add the potatoes and cook, stirring, for 4 minutes. Pour in the water and season with the salt and ground pepper, then cover and bring to a simmer. Cook until the potatoes are very soft (about 20 minutes).

With a fork mash the potatoes to a puree against the side of the pot, or use a potato masher. Add the reserved sausage to the pot and cook for 5 minutes. Increase the heat, bring to a boil, add the greens, and cook, uncovered, until tender (about 3 minutes). Do not overcook. Serve hot.

Serves 4 to 6.

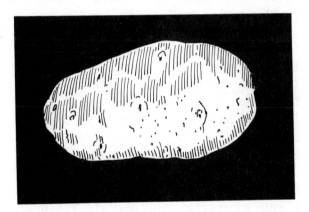

Chick-pea Soup with Ham

There are many variations of soup with legumes and ham or sausage. Here is an adaptation of a fairly standard version. Several variations follow. Use dried legumes and schedule the cooking time accordingly. The flavor of all legume and ham soups is enhanced by adding a ham bone (trimmed of all visible fat) and substituting vegetable stock for part or all of the water. Serve this soup with a green salad, thick slices of crusty Italian bread, and chilled beer or light red wine.

1 pound dried chick-peas, rinsed and picked over
1 tablespoon olive oil
2 carrots, diced
2 medium onions, chopped coarsely
3 cloves garlic, minced
2 medium potatoes, diced
2 fresh tomatoes, peeled and chopped
1/4 pound cooked ham or turkey ham, minced
1 bay leaf
2 tablespoons minced parsley
1/2 teaspoon salt
1/2 teaspoon freshly ground black pepper
12 cups water, preferably part of it Vegetable Stock (page 147)

Place the chick-peas in a saucepan, add water to cover, cover the pot, and bring to a boil over high heat. Remove from the heat and let stand for about 15 minutes, then drain and discard the water. Set aside.

In a large soup pot over medium heat, warm the oil. Add the carrots, onions, garlic, and potatoes and sauté until the vegetables are soft. Add the reserved chick-peas, tomatoes, ham, bay leaf, parsley, salt, ground pepper, the water, and stock. Cover and simmer until the chick-peas are tender (about 3 hours). Taste and adjust the seasoning, if desired. Discard the bay leaf. Serve hot.

Serves 8.

Variations

Split Pea Soup with Marjoram. Substitute 1 pound split peas, green or yellow (or a mixture), for the chick-peas. Omit the bay leaf and add 2 teaspoons dried marjoram. Sprinkle each serving with a little more marjoram.

Lentil Soup with Bacon. Substitute 1 pound lentils for the chick-peas. Substitute 2 slices turkey bacon, chopped fine, for the ham; sauté it first and drain it on paper towels. Drain the fat from the pan and then proceed with the vegetables. Simmer the soup for about 1 hour.

Tuscan Bean Soup. Omit the bay leaf; substitute 1 tablespoon minced fresh basil (*or* 1 teaspoon dried basil) and 1 teaspoon minced fresh sage (*or* 1/2 teaspoon rubbed dried sage). Omit the potatoes. Simmer for about 3 hours. Serve garnished with additional minced parsley and a squeeze of lemon juice over the top. Serves 6 or 7.

Hearty Bean and Sausage Soup. Substitute 1 pound dried navy beans for the chick-peas; increase the water by 2 cups. Omit the ham. Simmer for about 3 hours. About 15 minutes before serving, add 1/2 cup broken thin spaghetti and 3 smoked hotdogs, preferably chicken or turkey, sliced thin. Cook until the spaghetti is tender. Taste and adjust the seasoning. Garnish with chopped parsley. Serves 10.

Poule au Pot

Here is the chicken form of the Pot au Feu. You can use some of the cooked meat for other purposes (leave the bones in until the very end, since they add considerable flavor) and you can strain off some of the stock for use in another recipe. Since chicken stock is quite perishable, either use it within 2 days or freeze it. With this soup serve a salad of romaine with orange slices and raisins and Creamy Orange Dressing (page 150), and thick slices of crusty whole-grain French bread.

1 stewing chicken (about 4 pounds), cut into
    pieces
3 large onions, chopped
4 carrots, sliced
3 cloves garlic, minced
8 cups water
4 stalks celery, cut into 2-inch lengths, with tops
    chopped
4 medium potatoes, cubed
2 bay leaves
6 black peppercorns
1 teaspoon dried thyme
1 teaspoon dried oregano
Minced parsley, for garnish (optional)

In a large soup pot over medium-high heat, brown the chicken pieces a few at a time. Remove them to a plate and set aside. Drain off most of the fat.

Reduce the heat to medium and add the onions, carrots, and garlic. Sauté until the onions soften somewhat. Reduce the heat to low and slowly add the water. Then add the reserved chicken pieces and the celery, potatoes, bay leaves, peppercorns, thyme, and oregano. Cover and simmer until the chicken is tender (about 1 1/2 hours).

Strain the chicken stock into a large container and chill until the fat rises to the top and can be skimmed off. Reserve 2 cups for another use. Remove the chicken skin and bones; cut the chicken into small pieces and return them to the soup pot. Discard the bay leaves. Stir in the skimmed stock, bring to a boil, and adjust the seasoning, if necessary. Garnish with the minced parsley, if desired, and serve hot.

Serves 6 to 8.

Variation

Chicken Soup with Dumplings. After you have cut up the cooked chicken and reheated the broth, prepare the dough for Parsley Dumplings (page 152) and drop 8 mounds onto the boiling liquid. Cover tightly and cook for 15 minutes. Do not lift the lid. Serves 8.

Chicken Soup with Garden Vegetables. After you have reheated the broth, add 1 green bell pepper, cut into small pieces; 1 cup fresh or frozen peas; 1 cup cut green beans; and 1 cup fresh corn kernels, cut from the cob. Simmer until the vegetables are cooked. Serves 8 to 10.

Chicken Gumbo. Omit the potatoes. After you have reheated the broth, add 1 small red bell pepper, chopped; 1 package (10 ounces) frozen cut okra; 1 package (10 ounces) frozen corn kernels; 1 1/2 cups chopped tomato, fresh or canned; and 1 cup cooked long-grain white or brown rice. Serves 8 to 10.

Mulligatawny Soup

This colorful and exotic soup, with an unusual and zesty flavor, comes from India. Like other such favorite ethnic soups, it has many different versions. Broadly defined, it is a soup with a chicken base strongly seasoned with curry. Some recipes include tomatoes. This version adds the extra nutrition of legumes. Serve it with whole wheat pita bread.

2 whole chicken breasts (about 1 1/2 pounds each), skinned and halved
1 tablespoon curry powder
1 medium onion, chopped
1 clove garlic, minced
2 tablespoons chopped parsley
3/4 cup brown rice
2 tablespoons regular lentils
2 tablespoons dried split peas, yellow or green
2 tablespoons chopped green bell pepper
2 tablespoons chopped red bell pepper
1/2 teaspoon salt
1/2 teaspoon freshly ground white pepper
1 1/2 cups chopped tart apple *or* 1/2 cup chopped dried apple
2 tablespoons red lentils
1/2 cup plain nonfat yogurt

Place the chicken breasts in a large saucepan or soup pot and add water to cover. Add the curry, onion, garlic, and parsley. Cover and bring to a boil, then reduce the heat and simmer until the chicken is tender (about 30 minutes). Remove the chicken from the stock and set aside to cool.

Add enough water to the stock to make 6 cups. Bring it to a boil, and add the rice, brown lentils, split peas, bell peppers, salt, ground pepper, and apple. Simmer gently.

When the chicken is cool enough to handle, remove it from the bones, dice it, and add it to the pot. Cook the soup for 35 minutes more, then stir in the red lentils and continue cooking until the rice is done and the legumes are tender (about 10 minutes). Stir in the yogurt. Taste and adjust the seasonings and serve at once.

Serves 8.

Variation

Mulligatawny Soup with Tomatoes. Substitute 1/4 cup each diced carrot and celery for the lentils and split peas. Omit the yogurt and stir in 1 1/2 cups fresh or canned tomatoes and cook until thoroughly heated.

Canadian Country Supper Soup

Here is a hearty turkey soup with unusual ingredients. Use adzuki beans if possible. Serve this soup with thick slices of whole wheat bread.

3/4 cup small dried red beans, preferably adzuki
1 pound ground uncooked turkey *or* 2 cups minced cooked turkey
1 large onion, chopped
1 large clove garlic, minced
5 cups water
1 can (16 ounces) crushed tomatoes
1 cup Tomato Sauce (page 147)
1/2 small head cabbage, chopped
3 carrots, sliced
3 stalks celery, sliced
1/2 cup long-grain brown rice
1 teaspoon salt
1 bay leaf
1 teaspoon dried thyme
1/2 teaspoon dried marjoram
1/2 teaspoon freshly ground black pepper

Cover the beans with boiling water and let stand for 2 to 3 hours.

In a soup pot or large saucepan over medium heat, sauté the turkey, onion, and garlic, stirring well, until the onion is transparent. Drain off the fat.

Drain the beans and add them to the pot along with the remaining ingredients. Mix well, cover, and bring to a boil, then reduce the heat and simmer until the beans are done (about 1 1/2 hours). Serve at once.

Serves 8.

Variation

Turkey and Barley Soup. Substitute 3/4 cup lentils for the red beans, 2 cups fresh or frozen corn for the cabbage, and 1/2 cup pearl barley for the rice. Just before serving, stir in 1/4 cup dry sherry and garnish with chopped parsley.

Sopa de Vigília

Unlike many Mediterranean seafood stews and chowders, this Spanish soup is made with fish alone. According to tradition, meat is not eaten on Friday in Spain, hence the name Friday Soup. Serve it with a fresh green salad and lots of crusty French bread.

1 tablespoon olive oil
1/2 pound cod, cut in bite-sized pieces
1 large onion, chopped coarsely
1 clove garlic, crushed
1 slice white bread, crusts removed, diced
8 tomatoes, peeled and chopped, *or* 2 cups canned tomatoes, peeled and chopped
6 cups Fish Stock (page 146), heated, or water
1/2 cup short-grain brown rice
1 small cauliflower, separated into florets
1/2 teaspoon salt
1/2 teaspoon freshly ground black pepper

In a heavy saucepan or soup pot over medium heat, warm the oil. Add the cod, onion, and garlic and sauté for about 5 minutes. Add the diced bread and sauté for 2 minutes. Stir in the tomatoes, reduce the heat, and simmer for several minutes.

Add the stock, bring to a boil, and stir in the rice. Simmer for about 30 minutes; then add the cauliflower, salt, and ground pepper. Simmer until the rice is cooked. Serve immediately.

Serves 6.

Variation

Curried Fish Soup. Instead of cod, substitute 1/2 pound fish fillets, such as grouper or monkfish, skinned and cut into 1-inch cubes. Omit the bread. Sauté 1 tablespoon curry powder for about 1 minute. Just before serving, stir in 1/4 cup evaporated skimmed milk. Heat thoroughly but do not boil.

Bourride

This wonderful Provençal fish soup is traditionally served with *aïoli*, a garlic mayonnaise. Here is a potent but leaner version. The bourride should be served in a large bowl, with a slice of toasted French bread, called a *croûte*, on the bottom, a piece of fish on it, the soup ladled over the top, and a dollop of *aïoli* over all. This meal is somewhat complicated to prepare, but well worth the effort.

3/4 cup finely chopped onion
1 cup finely chopped celery
1 cup finely chopped leek
2 cloves garlic, minced
1 teaspoon ground saffron
1 bay leaf
1 cup dry white wine
2 cups cubed peeled potato
4 cups Fish Stock (page 146)
1/8 teaspoon cayenne pepper
Salt and freshly ground black pepper, to taste
4 pounds of at least 3 kinds of firm, white fish
    fillets, such as haddock, porgy, cod, sole, perch,
    rockfish, pollack, or halibut, cut into 2-inch
    pieces
8 slices French bread

Slender Aïoli

1 tablespoon fine dried bread crumbs
4 cloves garlic, chopped coarsely
3/4 cup reduced-fat mayonnaise
3/4 cup plain nonfat yogurt
1 tablespoon lemon juice

In a large saucepan over high heat, combine the onion, celery, leek, garlic, saffron, bay leaf, wine, potato, stock, cayenne, salt, and ground pepper. Bring to a boil, then reduce the heat and simmer for 30 minutes.

Meanwhile, prepare the *aïoli*. In a small bowl combine the bread crumbs and garlic and mash them to a smooth paste. Stir in the mayonnaise, yogurt, and lemon juice. Set aside.

Puree the cooked soup in the food processor until smooth. Place the fish pieces in the bottom of the saucepan, pour in the pureed soup, and simmer until the fish is cooked (about 5 minutes).

Toast the French bread by placing it in a 325 degree F oven for about 15 minutes on each side.

Transfer the cooked fish to a heated serving dish or tureen. Whisk 1 cup of the *aïoli* into the hot soup. Heat thoroughly but do not boil. Serve as described above, putting a dab of the remaining *aïoli* on each serving and passing the rest.

Serves 8.

Sicilian Fish Soup

This is one of many versions of Mediterranean fish soup. Serve this hearty family fare with a salad of marinated cooked vegetables (such as broccoli, cauliflower, and green beans) on a bed of greens, and thick slices of Italian bread.

1 tablespoon olive oil
1 cup coarsely chopped onion
1 cup chopped carrot
1/2 cup chopped green bell pepper
3 cloves garlic, crushed in a garlic press
1 can (28 ounces) Italian plum tomatoes, chopped, with juice
1 cup water
1/2 cup white wine
3 cups diced peeled potato
1 teaspoon fennel seeds
1/2 teaspoon salt
1/2 teaspoon freshly ground black pepper
1 tablespoon Italian Herb Blend (page 150)
2 pounds haddock fillets, fresh or frozen, cut into 2-inch pieces
Freshly grated Parmesan cheese, for garnish (optional)

In a heavy soup pot or large saucepan over medium heat, warm the oil. Add the onion, carrot, bell pepper, and garlic. Sauté until the onion is soft. Add the tomatoes, water, wine, potato, fennel, salt, and ground pepper. Simmer, covered, for 35 minutes.

Add the herb blend and fish and cook until the fish flakes when tested with a fork (about 10 minutes). Ladle into warm soup bowls and sprinkle each portion with a little cheese, if desired.

Serves 8.

Variations

For both variations, omit the fennel seeds and herb blend. Substitute 1 bottle (8 ounces) clam juice for the water and 1/4 cup chopped parsley for the cheese garnish.

Manhattan Fish Chowder. Add 1 tablespoon Worcestershire sauce, 1 teaspoon dried thyme, 1/2 teaspoon Hot Pepper Sauce (page 148), and 2 bay leaves with the tomatoes.

Corn and Crab Chowder. Add 1/2 cup chopped red bell pepper to the sautéed vegetables. Substitute 2 cups fresh lumb crabmeat for the fish. Stir 1/8 teaspoon red pepper flakes and 2 cups fresh or frozen corn kernels into the chowder. Serves 6.

Simple Bouillabaisse

The classic version of this famous Provençal sea-food stew is a complicated combination of many different ingredients. Like many famous and popular dishes, the possibilities are almost limitless and the versions numerous. This particular one is quick and simple, with fewer calories and less time needed for preparation. It is complemented by Rouille, a fiery chile *aïoli*. Serve this dish with dry white wine.

1 tablespoon olive oil
1 cup sliced carrot
1 cup sliced celery
1 cup sliced red onion
1 cup sliced fresh fennel
2 cups chopped peeled tomato
1 clove garlic, minced
1/4 teaspoon ground saffron
8 cups Fish Stock (page 146)
2 bay leaves
1 teaspoon dried thyme
1/2 teaspoon fennel seeds, crushed
1 firm white fish, such as halibut, red snapper, bass, haddock, or cod, cut into 1-inch pieces
1 pound scallops
24 shrimp, peeled and deveined
6 to 8 slices French bread
Olive oil, for French bread
1 clove garlic, for French bread
1 cup Rouille (page 148)

Prepare the Rouille and set aside.

In a 6-quart soup pot over medium-high heat, warm the 1 tablespoon olive oil. Sauté the carrot, celery, onion, and fresh fennel for about 5 minutes. Reduce the heat to medium-low and stir in the tomato, minced garlic, and saffron. Cook, stirring, for about 5 minutes.

Add the stock, bay leaves, thyme, and fennel seeds. Cover, reduce the heat to low, and simmer for about 30 minutes. Stir in the fish, scallops, and shrimp. Cover and simmer until the seafood is tender (5 to 7 minutes). Discard the bay leaves.

While the vegetables are cooking, prepare the *croûtes*: Toast the French bread in a 325 degree oven for 15 minutes on each side; brush with the olive oil, then rub with the garlic clove. Just before serving, thin the Rouille with 2 to 3 tablespoons of the soup stock.

To serve the soup, place a *croûte* in the bottom of each bowl and ladle the soup over it. Pass the Rouille separately.

Serves 6.

Australian Crab and Asparagus Soup

This is an elegant soup, handsome to look at, rich in interesting flavors. Serve it with thin slices of homemade white and rye bread.

1 tablespoon canola oil
1 cup chopped onion
1 cup chopped celery, with tops
1 large carrot, diced
2 cloves garlic, minced
2 shallots, minced
2 tablespoons all-purpose flour
4 cups skim milk
1 cup water
1/4 cup dry sherry
1/2 cup long-grain white rice
1 teaspoon Worcestershire sauce
1 bay leaf
1 teaspoon dried thyme
1/2 teaspoon salt
1/2 teaspoon freshly ground white pepper
1/2 teaspoon grated lemon zest
1 1/2 cups fresh lump crabmeat *or* 8 ounces frozen crab meat, defrosted, well drained, and flaked
1 1/2 cups sliced asparagus spears

In a large saucepan over medium heat, warm the oil. Sauté the onion, celery, carrot, garlic, and shallots, stirring occasionally, until the vegetables are soft (about 5 minutes). Sprinkle with the flour and stir quickly to combine. Add the milk, stirring constantly, and cook until the sauce is smooth.

Add the water, sherry, rice, Worcestershire, bay leaf, thyme, salt, ground pepper, and lemon zest. Bring to a boil; then reduce the heat to low and simmer for about 30 minutes. Stir in the crab and asparagus. Cover the pan and cook, stirring occasionally, until the soup is thickened and the asparagus is cooked. Discard the bay leaf and serve.

Serves 6.

Seafood Gumbo

This spicy and hearty southern soup is warming in every way. It is thick in consistency, full of vegetables and shellfish. Serve it with a mixed green salad and Triple Wheat Biscuits (page 152).

1/4 cup all-purpose flour
2 tablespoons canola oil
1 cup chopped onion
1/2 cup chopped celery
2 large cloves garlic, minced
1 large green bell pepper, chopped
2 teaspoons Cajun Herb and Spice Mix (page 151)
10 cups warm water
2 cups sliced fresh or frozen okra
1 cup Tomato Sauce (page 147)
1 cup long-grain brown rice
1/2 teaspoon salt
1 pound fresh shrimp, peeled and deveined
1/2 pound fresh lump crabmeat, flaked
1 tablespoon dried parsley
1/4 cup chopped green onion tops

In a heavy soup pot over medium heat, combine the flour and oil. Cook, stirring constantly, until the roux is the color of a copper penny (10 to 15 minutes). Add the onion, celery, garlic, bell pepper, and herb mix and continue to cook, stirring constantly, until the vegetables are tender. Be careful not to burn the roux.

Gradually stir in the warm water, blending well. Add the okra and Tomato Sauce and bring to a boil. Stir in the rice. Reduce the heat to medium-low, cover, and simmer, stirring occasionally, for 1 to 1 1/2 hours. Add the salt, shrimp, and crabmeat. Bring the gumbo to a boil, reduce the heat to low, and simmer for another 10 minutes. Add the parsley and green onion and simmer for 5 minutes longer. Serve immediately.

Serves 6.

New England Clam Chowder

This easy version of a classic soup is tasty and lean. Serve the soup with a fresh green salad and Skinny Corn Bread (page 152).

2 cans (6 1/2 ounces each) minced clams, undrained
2 slices turkey bacon
1 1/2 cups finely chopped onion
1 large clove garlic, minced
1 small carrot, sliced
2 stalks celery, sliced, with tops chopped
4 cups diced peeled red potato (about 1 1/2 pounds)
1 teaspoon dried thyme
2 bottles (8 ounces each) clam juice
3 tablespoons all-purpose flour
2 cups Fish Stock (page 146)
1 can (12 ounces) evaporated skimmed milk
Freshly ground pepper, to taste
Chopped parsley, for garnish

Drain the clams, reserving the liquid; set aside.

In a large Dutch oven over medium heat, fry the bacon, onion, and garlic for about 5 minutes. Add the carrot and celery and sauté for 5 minutes longer. Drain off any fat. Add the reserved clam liquid, potato, thyme, and clam juice. Bring to a boil, cover, reduce the heat to low, and simmer until the potato is tender (about 20 minutes).

Puree 2 cups of the potato mixture, including the bacon strips, in a food processor. Return the puree to the pot and stir well. Stir in the reserved clams.

Measure the flour into a 4-cup measure and slowly add the stock, whisking until smooth. Add this to the pot and cook, stirring constantly, until thickened. Mix in the evaporated milk and ground pepper. Garnish with the parsley and serve.

Serves 4 to 6.

Caribbean Gazpacho with Scallops

This chilled soup has a zesty flavor. It is good with toasted tortillas, broken into chips.

12 ounces bay scallops
1/2 cup minced parsley
3 tablespoons lemon juice
4 cups chopped peeled tomato
1 1/2 cups tomato juice
1/2 avocado, chopped
1 cup chopped green bell pepper
1 cup chopped red bell pepper
1/2 cup chopped onion
2 large cloves garlic, minced
1 teaspoon Hot Pepper Sauce (page 148)
1 cup plain nonfat yogurt

Blanch the scallops in boiling water for 1 minute. Drain well, cut them into 3/4-inch pieces, and place in a large bowl. Stir in the parsley and lemon juice.

In a food processor combine the tomato, tomato juice, avocado, bell peppers, onion, garlic, and Hot Pepper Sauce. Pulsing on and off, process until coarsely chopped.

Add to the scallop mixture and refrigerate for at least 2 hours.

To serve, ladle into shallow soup bowls. Top with spoonfuls of yogurt.

Serves 4.

Southwest Vegetable Chowder

This mild chowder combines some favorite south-western flavors. If you want more heat, sauté 1/2 jalapeño pepper, minced, with the vegetables. Serve this soup with Skinny Corn Bread (page 152), or corn tortillas, baked slightly and cut into wedges. Chilled beer makes a fine accompaniment.

1 tablespoon canola oil
2 large onions, chopped
2 stalks celery, with leaves, chopped
1 medium carrot, diced
1 small red bell pepper, diced
1 small green bell pepper, diced
2 tablespoons all-purpose flour
5 cups Vegetable Stock (page 147) *or* Root Vege-
    table Stock (page 147)
4 cups water
3 large potatoes, unpeeled and cubed
2 1/2 teaspoons dry mustard
1 teaspoon dried marjoram
1/2 teaspoon freshly ground white pepper
3 cups corn kernels, fresh or frozen
1/2 cup shredded reduced-fat sharp Cheddar
    cheese
1 can (4 ounces) chopped green chiles, drained
3/4 teaspoon Tabasco sauce
Salt and freshly ground black pepper, to taste

In a large soup pot over medium heat, warm the oil. Sauté the onions, celery, carrots, and bell peppers, stirring frequently, until the onions are soft (about 5 minutes). Stir in the flour and cook, stirring, until incorporated. Gradually stir in the stock and the water; bring to a boil, stirring constantly. Cook until thickened and smooth.

Add the potatoes, mustard, marjoram, and ground pepper. Reduce the heat to low and simmer for 10 minutes. Stir in the corn and cook until the potatoes and corn are tender.

If desired, puree the soup in a food processor along with almost all the cheese. I prefer to mash some of the vegetables with a fork against the side of the pot, then add all but 2 tablespoons cheese and the green chiles. Heat, stirring, for about 5 minutes. Do not boil. Add the Tabasco; taste and add salt and ground pepper, if needed. Serve at once.

Serves 8.

Soupe au Pistou

This classic Provençal soup is popular all over France. It comes in many versions, of which two are given here. Serve it with thick slices of French bread and hearty red wine. The *pistou* is, of course, the French version of pesto.

2 tablespoons olive oil
1/2 cup chopped leek
1 medium potato, diced
1 cup diced carrot
1 cup fresh or frozen lima beans
1 1/2 cups sliced fresh green beans
1 small zucchini, diced
1/2 cup fresh or frozen peas
2 ripe tomatoes, peeled and chopped
6 cups Vegetable Stock (page 147)
1/4 cup shells, elbow macaroni, or broken
    spaghettini
Salt and freshly ground black pepper, to taste

Pistou

3 cloves garlic
1/4 cup chopped fresh basil *or* 2 1/2 tablespoons
    dried basil
1 tablespoon Crushed Tomatoes (page 148) or
    tomato paste
2 tablespoons freshly grated Parmesan cheese
2 tablespoons olive oil

In a large soup pot over medium heat, warm the oil. Sauté the leek until tender. Add the potato, carrot, lima beans, green beans, zucchini, peas, tomatoes, and stock; simmer, uncovered, for about 15 minutes. Increase the heat to high, bring to a rapid boil, and stir in the pasta. Cook until the pasta is done and the vegetables are tender. Taste and season with the salt and ground pepper.

Meanwhile, prepare the Pistou. With a mortar and pestle or a heavy bowl and a wooden spoon, mash the garlic and basil to a paste. Work in the tomatoes and the cheese, then stir in the oil until smooth.

Thin the Pistou with 1/4 cup of the soup stock and stir some of it into the soup. Serve the soup and pass the rest of the Pistou separately.

Serves 4 to 6.

Variation

Classic Soupe au Pistou. Cook 1/4 cup dried white beans in boiling water to cover for 2 minutes, then let soak for 1 hour. Drain and cover with fresh water, then simmer until almost tender (about 1 1/2 hours). Add to the soup with the vegetables.

Garden Vegetables and Millet Soup

Here's a chance to try millet, rich in vitamins and minerals and worthy of more attention in the kitchen. Serve this colorful soup with a salad and hearty whole wheat bread.

1/2 cup millet
1 1/2 cups water
Dash salt and freshly ground black pepper
1 tablespoon olive oil
1 large onion, diced
3 cups Vegetable Stock (page 147)
2 carrots, diced
1 large potato, diced
2 stalks celery, with tops, chopped
1 medium zucchini, chopped
1 cup cut green beans
2 medium tomatoes, chopped
1 bay leaf
1 teaspoon dried basil
1/2 teaspoon dried thyme
1 cup shredded spinach
1 cup skim milk

In a heavy saucepan over medium heat, lightly toast the millet for about 5 minutes. Let cool slightly, then add the water, salt, and ground pepper. Cover and cook for about 20 minutes. Remove from the heat and let stand for 10 minutes.

Meanwhile, in a large saucepan or small soup pot over medium heat, warm the oil. Sauté the onion until soft (about 5 minutes). Stir in the stock, carrots, potato, celery, zucchini, beans, tomatoes, bay leaf, basil, and thyme. Reduce the heat, cover, and simmer for about 30 minutes.

Stir in the spinach, toasted millet mixture, and milk. Simmer for 5 minutes. Discard the bay leaf before serving.

Serves 6.

Barley and Spinach Soup with Yogurt

This Middle Eastern soup is good with whole wheat pita bread, toasted with sesame seeds and broken into pieces.

7 cups Root Vegetable Stock (page 147)
1/2 cup pearl barley
1 package (10 ounces) leaf spinach *or* 1 package (10 ounces) frozen spinach
1 tablespoon olive oil
1 medium onion, chopped fine
2 cloves garlic, minced
2 tablespoons cornstarch
3 tablespoons water
2 cups plain nonfat yogurt
1/2 teaspoon salt
1/2 teaspoon freshly ground white pepper
2 tablespoons finely chopped fresh mint *or* 4 teaspoons dried mint, for garnish

In a soup pot or saucepan over high heat, bring the stock to a boil. Add the barley and simmer, covered, until tender (about 1 hour).

Remove the stems from the leaf spinach and cut the leaves crosswise into 1/2-inch strips. (If using frozen, defrost somewhat and slice lengthwise through the spinach.) Add to the barley and simmer for 3 minutes.

Meanwhile, in a nonstick skillet over medium heat, warm the oil. Sauté the onion and garlic until soft but not browned. Blend the cornstarch and water until smooth, stir in the salt, ground pepper, and yogurt, and add to the onion mixture. Reduce the heat and cook, stirring, until the mixture thickens. Stir into the spinach mixture and cook, stirring, for about 5 minutes. Serve immediately in warm bowls, garnished with the chopped mint.

Serves 4.

Minestrone

This is probably the most famous soup of Italy and, like most traditional dishes, comes with many variations. This hearty version should be served with thick slices of crusty garlic bread and hearty red wine.

1 cup dried red kidney beans, rinsed
3 cups boiling water
1 tablespoon olive oil
1 large leek, chopped, *or* 1 large onion, chopped
1 large clove garlic, minced
2 medium carrots, chopped
1 large potato, diced
1 cup chopped celery
1 can (16 ounces) whole tomatoes or 4 ripe tomatoes, peeled and chopped
6 cups water
6 cups Root Vegetable Stock (page 147)
1 tablespoon Italian Herb Blend (page 150)
1 teaspoon salt
1/2 teaspoon freshly ground black pepper
1/2 cup small shells, elbows, or spirals
2 cups shredded cabbage
1 medium zucchini, quartered and sliced thin
1/2 cup shredded part-skim mozzarella cheese, for garnish

In a large saucepan combine the beans and the boiling water; cook for 2 minutes, remove from the heat, and let stand for 1 hour.

Drain, then cover with 2 inches of fresh water. Bring to a boil, then reduce the heat and simmer until the beans are tender (about 1 1/2 hours), adding more water if needed. Drain the beans and set aside.

In a large soup pot over medium heat, warm the oil. Sauté the leek and garlic until soft; stir in the carrot, potato, and celery and sauté for 5 minutes. Stir in the drained beans, tomatoes, the 6 cups water, stock, herb blend, salt, and ground pepper. Bring to a boil, then reduce the heat, cover, and simmer for 30 minutes.

Return the soup to a boil and stir in the pasta. Cook for 10 minutes; then stir in the cabbage and zucchini and cook until the cabbage is tender (6 minutes).

Ladle the soup into heated bowls and garnish with the cheese. Serve hot.

Serves 10 to 12.

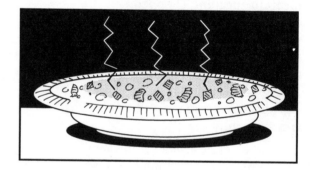

Multi-bean Soup

This substantial combination takes some time to assemble and cook, but it is worth every minute, and you end up with a hearty meal for a crowd.

1/4 cup dried navy beans
1/4 cup dried chick-peas
1/4 cup dried baby lima beans
1/4 cup dried black beans
1/4 cup dried red kidney beans
1/4 cup lentils
1/4 cup split green peas
1/4 cup split yellow peas
1 large onion, sliced
2 large carrots, cut into pieces
1 large green bell pepper, cut into pieces
1/2 cup celery pieces
1/2 cup chopped parsley
2 cloves garlic
6 cups Root Vegetable Stock (page 147)
2 teaspoons salt
1 teaspoon freshly ground white pepper
2 bay leaves
1 tablespoon Italian Herb Blend (page 150)
1/2 teaspoon dried winter savory
1/2 teaspoon ground coriander
2 cups chopped tomato

Wash and sort all the dried legumes. Place them in a large pan, cover with boiling water, and let them soak overnight. Drain, add water to cover, and cook until almost done (about 1 hour).

In a food processor chop the onion, carrots, bell pepper, celery, parsley, and garlic; add to the legumes with the stock and cook for 30 minutes. Stir in the remaining ingredients. Simmer for about 30 minutes.

Discard the bay leaves; taste and adjust the seasoning. If the soup is too thick, add more water.

Serves 8 to 10.

Cajun Corn Soup

This zesty and hearty vegetarian soup has a quantity of nutrition. You can easily double this recipe. Serve Skinny Corn Bread (page 152) with the soup.

1/4 cup dried black-eyed peas or soybeans, rinsed
1 tablespoon olive oil
1 large onion, chopped
1 green bell pepper, chopped
2 stalks celery, with tops, chopped
3 cloves garlic, minced
4 cups Vegetable Stock (page 147)
1 large tomato, chopped
2 bay leaves
1 teaspoon Cajun Herb and Spice Mix (page 151)
1/2 teaspoon dried rosemary
1/2 teaspoon dried basil
4 cups fresh or frozen corn kernels
1 cup shredded Swiss chard

Put the black-eyed peas in a saucepan and add water to cover 2 inches above the peas. Bring to a boil, reduce the heat, cover, and simmer for 10 minutes. Remove from the heat and allow to stand overnight.

Drain the peas; then cover with fresh water and simmer until the peas are tender and almost all the water is absorbed (about 1 hour).

In a large soup pot over medium heat, sauté the onion in the oil until it is light brown (about 8 minutes). Add the bell pepper, celery, and garlic and continue to sauté, stirring, for 5 minutes. Stir in the stock, tomato, bay leaves, spice mix, rosemary, and basil. Cover and simmer for 30 minutes.

Add the corn, Swiss chard, and cooked black-eyed peas. Stir to mix well, then simmer for 5 to 10 minutes. Discard the bay leaves before serving.

Serves 4.

Mexican Black Bean Soup

Here are long-cooking versions and a speedy one for this popular soup. Serve it with a mixed green salad and Skinny Corn Bread (page 152).

2 cups dried black beans, sorted and rinsed
8 cups water or a combination of water and
Vegetable Stock (page 147)
2 bay leaves
1 tablespoon olive oil
2 onions, chopped fine
2 large green bell peppers, chopped
2 carrots, chopped
4 cloves garlic, minced
2 medium potatoes, cubed
2 teaspoons ground cumin
1 teaspoon dried oregano
1 teaspoon dry mustard
1 teaspoon dried dill weed
1 can (4 ounces) chopped green chiles, undrained
1 teaspoon salt
Dash cayenne pepper
Juice of 1 lemon
1/2 cup plain low-fat yogurt

Measure the beans into a large saucepan, cover with water up to 2 inches above the beans, and bring to a boil over high heat. Reduce the heat and simmer for about 10 minutes. Let stand, covered, overnight.

Drain the beans, then add the 8 cups water (including some stock, if desired) and bay leaves. Bring to a boil and cook for about 2 hours, stirring occasionally.

In a large soup pot over medium heat, warm the oil. Sauté the onions, bell peppers, carrots, garlic, and potatoes until they are limp and slightly browned. Add the cumin, oregano, mustard, and dill; continue to cook, stirring, for about 5 minutes.

With a potato masher, mash some of the beans into a paste to thicken the soup somewhat. Add the vegetable mixture to the beans, along with the chiles, salt, cayenne, and lemon juice. Continue to simmer for 30 minutes or more. Discard the bay leaves. Taste and adjust the seasonings.

To serve, ladle the soup into warm bowls and top each serving with a dollop of yogurt.

Serves 8.

Variations

Black Bean Soup with Sausage. Omit the olive oil; sauté 1/2 pound hot Italian turkey sausage, in pieces. Drain on paper towels and drain off any fat. Then sauté the vegetables. Add the cooked sausage shortly before serving.

Quick Black Bean Soup. Substitute 2 cans (15 ounces each) black beans, drained and rinsed, for the dried beans. Reduce the water to 4 cups and stir in 1 can (16 ounces) crushed tomatoes. Sauté the vegetables as above, add 1 cup of the beans, and mash well. Then add the remaining beans and other ingredients and bring to a boil. Reduce the heat, cover, and simmer for about 15 minutes. This version should take 30 to 45 minutes in all.

Lentil and Orzo Soup

This interesting Italian soup is easily made and requires less cooking time than many others. The recipe makes a large quantity. You can freeze any leftover soup for another meal. Serve it with a salad of mixed greens, and thick slices of whole wheat bread or garlic bread.

6 cups water, divided
3 medium to large onions, chopped
3 carrots, sliced
3 stalks celery, with tops, chopped
1 cup lentils
1 small red bell pepper, chopped
1 tablespoon Italian Herb Blend (page 150)
1/2 teaspoon freshly ground black pepper
4 cups Root Vegetable Stock (page 147)
1 can (28 ounces) whole tomatoes, undrained and chopped
1 package (9 ounces) frozen Italian green beans
1 can (6 ounces) tomato paste
3 cloves garlic, minced
2 bay leaves
1 cup uncooked orzo
2 tablespoons white wine vinegar
Salt, to taste
Freshly grated Parmesan cheese, for garnish

In a large soup pot, combine 4 cups of the water, the onions, carrots, celery, lentils, bell pepper, herb blend, ground pepper, stock, tomatoes, beans, tomato paste, garlic, and bay leaves. Bring to a boil, then cover, reduce the heat, and simmer for 30 minutes, stirring occasionally.

Add the remaining 2 cups water, orzo, and vinegar. Cover and simmer until the lentils are tender (30 minutes or more), stirring occasionally.

Discard the bay leaves. Taste and add the salt, if needed; remember that the cheese garnish will add salt.

Ladle the soup into heated bowls and sprinkle with the cheese. Serve at once.

Serves 12.

Variation

White Bean Soup with Wheat Berries. Substitute 1 cup small dried white beans for the lentils. Substitute 1 cup soft wheat berries for the orzo. Both should be soaked for several hours before cooking, then drained. Cooking time for the beans is about 2 hours, and for the wheat berries approximately 45 minutes. Instead of the herb blend, use 2 teaspoons rubbed dried sage.

Barley and Apple Soup

This combination of ingredients makes an attractive soup. Choose firm, tart, red-skinned apples and be sure to wash and dry them well. Accompany the soup with Skinny Corn Bread (page 152) or Simple Garlic Bread (page 152).

1 tablespoon canola oil
2 large onions, sliced thin
3 stalks celery, with tops, chopped
3 1/2 cups Vegetable Stock (page 147)
1 1/2 cups apple cider or unsweetened apple juice
1/3 cup pearl barley
2 large carrots, diced
1 teaspoon dried thyme
1/4 teaspoon dried marjoram
1 large bay leaf
2 cups chopped unpeeled apple
1/4 cup minced parsley
1 tablespoon lemon juice
1/4 teaspoon salt

In a soup pot over medium heat, warm the oil. Add the onions and sauté for 5 minutes, stirring. Stir in the celery and continue to sauté, stirring, for another 5 minutes. Reduce the heat to medium-low, cover, and cook, stirring frequently, until the vegetables are golden brown (about 20 minutes).

Reduce the heat to low and add the stock, cider, barley, carrots, thyme, marjoram, and bay leaf. Cover and cook until the barley is tender (about 1 hour).

Add the apple, parsley, lemon juice, and salt. Cook until the apple is slightly soft (about 5 minutes). Discard the bay leaf and serve immediately.

Serves 4.

Gazpacho Andaluz

This famous chilled soup is a favorite all over the world. With its crouton garnish, it makes a complete meal. Serve with chilled light white wine.

2 large firm, ripe tomatoes, cut into wedges
1 medium green bell pepper, cubed
1 medium cucumber, sliced thick
2 tablespoons Crushed Tomatoes (page 148) or tomato paste
1/2 cup fine dried bread crumbs
1/4 teaspoon ground cumin
1 clove garlic, minced
1 tablespoon olive oil
3 tablespoons red wine vinegar
3 cups Vegetable Stock (page 147), chilled
1/2 teaspoon salt
1/3 teaspoon freshly ground black pepper

Garnish

1 small green bell pepper, minced
1 medium tomato, peeled and chopped fine
1 small cucumber, chopped
1 small onion, chopped
1 1/2 cups croutons, toasted

With a food processor, chop the garnish ingredients separately and place in individual serving dishes. Refrigerate.

Place the soup ingredients in a food processor or blender, in batches if necessary, and process until nearly smooth. Taste and adjust the seasoning if necessary. Chill for several hours.

Before serving, stir the soup thoroughly and pour into individual bowls. Pass the garnish ingredients separately.

Serves 4.

Hearty Salads and Sandwiches

The idea of a salad or a sandwich as a meal in itself is a modern one, growing out of the cooking traditions of the United States. You can find examples of the main-dish salad in other cuisines—the Middle Eastern tabouli and the French salade niçoise come to mind—but by and large this is our domain. An interesting form, very popular today, is the dish of grilled meat or fish, often marinated before grilling, served on a bed of greens. The possibilities for sandwich fillings, in pita breads, for example, or the open-faced sandwich, have led to a whole new way of thinking about the meal's main course.

The obvious advantage of such dishes is that they require very little cooking and thus are well suited to the warmer months of the year. These salads and sandwiches often use leftover foods and readily available, quickly prepared ingredients, making them a fine choice when time and energy are limited.

Try to use fresh ingredients wherever possible. Especially in a salad, freshness can make a significant difference in the flavor and texture of the meal. Remember too that many salads need to be kept cold before serving, and leftovers should be refrigerated as soon as possible.

Spicy Beef Salad

This "meat and potatoes" salad is served warm. Serve it with warm dinner rolls and light red wine.

1 teaspoon paprika
1/2 teaspoon dried oregano
1/2 teaspoon dried thyme
1/4 teaspoon cayenne
12 ounces beef tenderloin, all visible fat removed
20 small new potatoes, halved
1 cup orange sections
1 red bell pepper, cut into strips
1 head Boston lettuce or flame red-leaf lettuce

Dressing
1/3 cup orange juice
1 tablespoon cider vinegar
1 tablespoon canola oil
1 tablespoon snipped chives
1 teaspoon Dijon mustard
1 teaspoon minced peeled fresh ginger

In a 1-cup measure, combine the paprika, oregano, thyme, and cayenne. Rub the mixture into the beef on all sides.

In a large ovenproof skillet over high heat, sear the meat quickly on both sides. Reduce the heat to medium and add the potatoes. Transfer the pan to a 400 degree F oven and roast until the meat is cooked rare and the potatoes are tender (about 20 minutes). Remove the pan from the oven and slice the meat across the grain into very thin slices.

Mix the cooked potatoes, orange, and bell pepper in a large bowl. Mix the dry ingredients in a 1-cup measure. Pour over the vegetables and toss lightly.

To serve, arrange the lettuce leaves on a platter, the meat slices on top, and the vegetables over all.

Serves 4.

Asian Beef with Asparagus and Broccoli

This dish offers a delightful contrast of subtle flavors and textures. Serve it with homemade whole wheat or cornmeal rolls.

6 ounces Asian rice noodles, broken in half
1 piece (about 1 pound) flank steak or London broil, all visible fat removed
4 cups diagonally sliced fresh asparagus (2-inch pieces)
1 bunch broccoli, tender stems cut into rounds, florets cut into bite-sized pieces
Salad bowl lettuce, washed and spun dry

Ginger Dressing

1/3 cup low-sodium soy sauce
1/4 cup distilled white vinegar
2 tablespoons sesame oil
1 piece (1 1/2 inches) fresh ginger, peeled and grated
Dash sugar
1/4 teaspoon freshly ground white pepper

In a large saucepan cover the rice noodles with boiling water for about 5 minutes. Drain in a colander and set aside.

In a large nonstick skillet over high heat, sear the steak on both sides. Reduce the heat to medium and pan-fry until cooked rare. Remove to a platter or a large flat bowl.

Add the drained noodles to the skillet and fry until lightly browned. Cut the steak into very thin slices. Pile the noodles on top and set aside.

In the same saucepan used to soak the noodles, bring 6 cups slightly salted water to a boil. Add the asparagus and blanch for 30 seconds. Remove with a slotted spoon and set aside to cool. Add the broccoli to the same water and blanch for about 45 seconds. Drain well and let cool.

Combine the dressing ingredients in a 2-cup measure, pour over the beef and noodles, and toss to combine. Add the vegetables and toss well.

Arrange the lettuce leaves around the edge of a platter and spoon the salad mixture over top. Serve at room temperature.

Serves 4 to 6.

Picadillo, Mexican Style

This is rather like a Mexican version of the sloppy joe, eaten with lettuce leaves. Serve it with corn tortillas, baked and cut into wedges or broken into chips, and chilled beer. Leftover picadillo could be served the next day, slightly warmed, in pita bread with shredded romaine.

1 pound lean ground beef
2 large onions, chopped fine
1 large green bell pepper, chopped fine
3 cloves garlic, minced
1 mild green chile (New Mexican or poblano), seeded and minced
1 cup Tomato Sauce (page 147)
2 medium potatoes, diced
2 tart apples, unpeeled, chopped
1/3 cup raisins
2 teaspoons dried oregano
1 teaspoon dried cumin
Dash ground cloves
1 head romaine lettuce
1 lime, cut into wedges
Chopped cilantro, for garnish

In a large nonstick skillet over medium heat, brown the beef, breaking it up with a wooden spoon or scraper. Add the onions, bell pepper, garlic, and chile; sauté, stirring often, until the beef is browned and the onion is translucent. Drain off any fat.

Stir in the Tomato Sauce, potatoes, apples, raisins, oregano, cumin, and cloves. Cover and simmer for about 30 minutes.

Meanwhile, separate the lettuce leaves and place them around the edge of a serving platter. Spoon the picadillo into the center of the platter. Have your guests help themselves by spooning some of the meat onto a lettuce leaf, squeezing lime juice and sprinkling cilantro over it, then rolling up the lettuce leaf.

Serves 8.

Greek Salad in Pita Bread

Here is a fast, easy recipe for the microwave. Be sure to cover the pitas with paper towels while they are in the oven, otherwise they will be soggy. Serve them with hearty red wine.

1/2 pound extra-lean ground beef
2 cups diced peeled eggplant
1/4 cup chopped onion
1/4 cup chopped green bell pepper
1 clove garlic, minced
1 large ripe tomato, diced (about 1 cup)
1/4 cup chopped cucumber
1/4 cup sliced Greek or ripe black olives
1 tablespoon fresh lemon juice
1 teaspoon chopped fresh oregano *or* 1/4 teaspoon dried oregano
1/4 teaspoon salt
1/4 teaspoon freshly ground black pepper
4 whole wheat pita breads, halved
1/2 cup plain low-fat yogurt

Crumble the beef in a 2-quart casserole. Add the eggplant, onion, bell pepper, and garlic. Cover with waxed paper and microwave on high (100%) until the beef is browned (4 to 5 minutes), stirring once after 2 minutes. Drain.

Add the tomato, cucumber, olives, lemon juice, oregano, salt, and ground pepper. Stir well.

Divide the mixture among the pita halves (about 1/2 cup for each). Arrange the pitas, side by side, in an 11- by 7- by 2-inch baking dish. Cover with 4 damp paper towels. Microwave on high for 3 to 4 minutes, rotating the dish a half turn after 1 1/2 minutes, if necessary.

Top each pita with 1 tablespoon yogurt. Serve immediately.

Serves 4.

Salade de Jambon et Persille

This colorful salad combines the fresh vegetables of late summer with the French combination of ham and parsley. Serve with whole-grain French bread and dry white wine.

2 teaspoons Herbes de Provence (page 150) or Fines Herbes (page 151)
3/4 cup Creamy Vinaigrette (page 149)
3/4 pound cooked ham or turkey ham, cut in a 1/2-inch-thick slice
2 ounces reduced-fat Jarlsberg or Swiss cheese
4 celery stalks, with the celery heart, diced fine
1 medium zucchini, quartered, then sliced
2 cups diced peeled ripe tomato
1 cup cooked corn kernels
1 small red or green bell pepper, chopped
3/4 cup finely chopped parsley
1 cup finely chopped sweet onion
Lettuce leaves, for serving

Stir the herbs into the Creamy Vinaigrette. Let it stand while preparing the salad.

Cut the ham into 1/2-inch cubes and place in a large salad bowl. Cut the cheese into 1/4-inch cubes and add to the bowl.

Add the celery, zucchini, tomato, corn, bell pepper, parsley, and onion; mix gently. Add the herbed vinaigrette and toss well. Serve on the lettuce leaves.

Serves 6.

Spinach, Apple, and Bacon Salad

For this tasty and colorful variation of the traditional spinach salad, choose red apples that are firm and tart. Serve this elegant dish with thin slices of French bread, lightly toasted, and chilled dry white wine.

4 slices turkey bacon
1/3 cup sliced almonds
1 pound fresh spinach, stems removed, leaves torn into bite-sized pieces
1/4 pound fresh mushrooms, sliced
2 medium apples, unpeeled, chopped
4 green onions, sliced thin
Creamy Vinaigrette (page 149)

In a large nonstick skillet over medium-high heat, sauté the bacon until browned and crisp. Drain it well on paper towels. Crumble and set aside.

Pour off the fat but do not wipe out the pan. Add the almonds and shake the pan until the nuts are slightly roasted. Remove the pan from the heat and set the nuts aside.

In a large salad bowl, combine the spinach, mushrooms, apples, and green onions; toss lightly. Add the reserved bacon and almonds and toss again. Pour the dressing over all and toss again before serving.

Serves 6.

Pasta Shells with Ham

This dish with an Italian flavor is simple and delicious. Serve it on a bed of lettuce with sliced tomatoes and with thick slices of Simple Garlic Bread (page 152) or Italian bread.

1/2 cup reduced-fat ricotta cheese
4 ounces Yogurt Cheese (page 150)
2 tablespoons lemon juice
1 tablespoon white wine vinegar
1/4 teaspoon salt
1/2 teaspoon freshly ground white pepper
1 pound pasta shells, spirals, or elbows
1 1/2 cups peas, fresh or frozen
1 1/2 cups diagonally sliced asparagus (2-inch pieces)
1 cup chopped cooked ham or turkey ham

In a large bowl mash the ricotta and Yogurt Cheese with a fork. Stir in the lemon juice, vinegar, salt, and ground pepper. Chill in the refrigerator.

Cook the pasta according to directions on page 46, remove it with a slotted spoon, and rinse with cold water.

In the same water add the peas and asparagus and blanch for 30 seconds. Remove with a slotted spoon and drain. Let cool.

Add the vegetables and ham to the chilled cheese mixture. Add the cooled pasta and toss lightly until well combined. Chill for 1 hour before serving.

Serves 8.

Variation

Tuna and Pasta Salad. Add 1 red bell pepper, seeded and chopped. Instead of the ham use 1 can (6 1/2 ounces) chunk tuna in water, drained and flaked.

Chicken Fajitas

This popular Mexican salad-sandwich offers a wonderful combination of flavors and textures.

10 to 12 ounces boneless, skinless chicken breasts
2 tablespoons fresh lime juice
1 clove garlic, crushed in a garlic press
1 cup cooked red kidney beans or 1 cup canned beans, rinsed
2 teaspoons olive oil
2 teaspoons white wine vinegar
Dick's Salsa (page 149), as needed
1 large onion, sliced thin
4 flour tortillas
1 cup shredded romaine lettuce
1 large ripe tomato, sliced thin
1/8 teaspoon ground cumin
1/2 cup plain low-fat yogurt
Chopped cilantro or parsley, for garnish

Cut the chicken into thin strips and place in a small bowl with the lime juice and garlic.

Mash the beans with the oil and vinegar. Add enough salsa to make a thick mixture.

Place the chicken and its marinade on a nonstick baking sheet and top with the onion slices; broil for about 3 minutes. Stir and continue broiling until the chicken is no longer pink inside (2 to 3 minutes).

Meanwhile, warm the tortillas by wrapping them in aluminum foil and placing them on the oven rack below the baking sheet.

To assemble the fajitas, fill each warm tortilla with 1/4 of the chicken, onion, bean mixture, shredded lettuce, and tomato. Stir the cumin into the yogurt and spoon it over the top. Garnish with the cilantro and serve additional salsa on the side.

Serves 4.

Thai Chicken and Noodles

This unusual salad combines warm chicken and noodles with grated vegetables. Use a food processor to grate the vegetables and the job is easy. Serve with crusty bread to soak up the marinade, and cold beer.

1/2 pound Asian rice noodles
1/4 cup minced parsley
1/4 cup lime juice
1/4 cup lemon juice
2 teaspoons low-sodium soy sauce
1/2 teaspoon red pepper flakes
1/2 teaspoon grated peeled fresh ginger
3 cloves garlic, minced
1 pound boneless, skinless chicken breasts
1 teaspoon canola oil
4 large radishes, grated
2 medium cucumbers, seeded and grated
1 small zucchini, grated
1 small yellow summer squash, grated
2 green onions, cut into 2-inch segments and
    shredded lengthwise

Break the noodles in half and place in a shallow glass dish. Pour boiling water over them and let stand 5 minutes. Drain into a colander and set aside.

Rinse the dish and wipe it. In it combine the parsley, lime juice, lemon juice, soy sauce, pepper flakes, fresh ginger, and garlic. Pound the chicken breasts to an even thickness (about 1/2 inch) with a mallet. Cut into thin strips and add to the dish, turning to coat the pieces with the marinade. Cover and marinate for 30 minutes, turning the pieces after 15 minutes.

In a large nonstick skillet over medium-high heat, warm the oil. Add the chicken, reserving the marinade, and sauté, stirring occasionally, until cooked through (about 10 minutes). Transfer to a plate. Add the drained noodles and sauté until lightly browned, stirring.

Put the noodles on a platter and arrange the grated radishes, cucumbers, zucchini, and summer squash over them. Add the reserved chicken marinade to the pan and boil for about 30 seconds. Stir in the chicken and mix well. Let it cool slightly, then arrange over the vegetables. Garnish with the green onions. Serve warm.

Serves 6.

Curried Chicken and Rice Salad

This colorful combination features some unusual textures. Serve with warm whole wheat pita bread.

1 cup cut fresh young green beans (1-inch pieces)
2 large tart red apples, chopped
2 cups chopped celery
1 cup thinly sliced green onion
1 can (5 ounces) sliced water chestnuts, drained
1/3 cup raisins
1/4 cup chopped unsalted peanuts
1/4 cup minced parsley
2 cups diced cooked chicken
3 cups cooked brown rice

Curry Dressing

1/3 cup white wine vinegar
2 tablespoons lemon juice
2 tablespoons canola oil
2 tablespoons plain nonfat yogurt
1 teaspoon Dijon mustard
2 teaspoons curry powder
Salt and freshly ground white pepper, to taste

Steam the beans until crisp-tender; drain thoroughly and allow to cool.

In a large salad bowl, combine the beans with the remaining ingredients. Mix well.

In a 4-cup measure whisk the vinegar, lemon juice, oil, yogurt, mustard, and curry powder until smooth. Add the salt and ground pepper, if desired.

Use as much dressing as needed to moisten the salad well. Serve on individual plates.

Serves 6.

Chicken Tabouli with Yogurt and Cumin Sauce

Tabouli (or tabbouleh) is a popular Middle Eastern combination. Adding cooked chicken has made this salad an all-time favorite in my house. Serve it with whole wheat pita bread and dry white wine.

1 cup coarse-grained bulgur
1 1/2 cups boiling water
1/2 teaspoon salt
1/4 cup fresh lemon juice
1/4 cup olive oil
1 1/2 teaspoons crushed garlic
1/2 cup chopped green onion, with green tops
1 cup tightly packed chopped parsley
2 small zucchini, quartered, then sliced
1 1/2 cups finely chopped cooked chicken
1/2 cup cooked chick-peas
2 medium tomatoes, chopped
Butterhead or bibb lettuce leaves, for serving
Chopped fresh mint (optional)
1 cup plain low-fat yogurt
1/4 teaspoon ground cumin

Measure the bulgur into a large salad or mixing bowl. Pour the boiling water over it, add the salt, stir well, and let stand for 20 minutes.

Pour the lemon juice and oil over the bulgur. Add the garlic, green onion, parsley, zucchini, chicken, and chick-peas; stir well. Chill the tabouli for several hours.

Just before serving, chop the tomatoes and stir them in. Arrange the salad on the lettuce leaves and garnish with the chopped mint, if desired. Combine the yogurt and cumin and serve it on the side.

Serves 6.

Chicken and Rice Waldorf Salad

This variation adds chicken and rice to an old favorite and cuts down the fat as well. Serve with thick slices of hearty whole wheat bread or with Triple Wheat Biscuits (page 152), and dry white wine.

2 cups diced cooked chicken
1 1/2 cups cooked brown rice
2 cups cubed unpeeled tart red apple
1 cup chopped celery
1 cup seedless red or green grapes, halved
Romaine lettuce leaves, for serving
3 tablespoons finely chopped toasted walnuts, for garnish

Dressing
2 tablespoons cold water
1/4 teaspoon unflavored gelatin
2 tablespoons white wine vinegar
2 tablespoons frozen apple juice concentrate, defrosted
1 tablespoon lemon juice
1 teaspoon vegetable oil
1/2 teaspoon dry mustard
1/2 cup plain low-fat yogurt

In a large bowl combine the chicken, rice, apple, celery, and grapes; toss lightly.

To prepare the dressing, measure the cold water into a small saucepan, sprinkle with the gelatin, and let stand for 1 minute. Cook over low heat, stirring, until the gelatin dissolves. Stir in the remaining dressing ingredients and whisk until smooth. Pour the dressing over the chicken mixture and toss lightly and thoroughly.

To serve, arrange the lettuce leaves on a large platter or individual plates, spoon the salad over, and garnish with the walnuts.

Serves 6.

Stuffed Zucchini Salad

Although the concept of stuffed vegetables comes from the Middle Eastern tradition, this salad has a Mexican-style stuffing. Serve it with baked corn tortillas or Skinny Corn Bread (page 152), and chilled beer.

3 medium zucchini (about 8 to 10 ounces each), halved lengthwise
1 ripe avocado, peeled and coarsely chopped
6 green onions, minced
2 stalks celery, chopped fine
1 green bell pepper, chopped
2 medium tomatoes, chopped
1 cup minced cooked chicken or turkey breast
Romaine lettuce leaves, shredded, for serving
1/2 cup shredded reduced-fat Monterey jack cheese

Dressing
1/2 cup Creamy Vinaigrette (page 149), or more as needed
2 teaspoons drained capers
1 teaspoon paprika
1/2 teaspoon ground cumin
1/4 teaspoon cayenne pepper

Parboil the zucchini until just tender (about 3 minutes). Let cool, then scoop out the flesh into a large bowl. Set the shells aside.

Chop the zucchini flesh coarsely, then add the avocado, green onions, celery, bell pepper, tomatoes, and chicken. Mix well.

In a 2-cup measure mix the dressing ingredients and blend well. Pour the dressing over the salad and stir to mix. Add more Creamy Vinaigrette, if needed.

Stuff the salad into the reserved zucchini shells. Serve them on the lettuce leaves and sprinkle with the cheese.

Serves 6.

Cold Turkey and Red Lentil Salad

Mediterranean flavors combine with cold turkey in this colorful dish. If you cannot find red lentils, use regular lentils, which you will have to cook for about 25 minutes. Serve the salad with thick slices of crusty Italian bread or whole wheat bread, and dry white wine.

2 cups red lentils
5 cups water
2 cups cooked brown rice
2 cups chopped turkey, mostly white meat
2 stalks celery, with tops, chopped
2 bunches watercress, chopped coarsely
1 clove garlic, minced
1/2 cup minced green onion
1/4 cup drained capers or chopped sour pickle
Lettuce leaves, for serving
1 large ripe tomato, cut into thin wedges
3 ounces goat cheese, for garnish

Dressing
1 cup Slim Yogurt Dressing (page 149)
2 tablespoons Turkey Stock (page 146) or Chicken Stock (page 146), or more as needed
1 teaspoon Herb and Pepper Mix (page 151)

In a large saucepan cover the lentils with the water. Bring to a boil and cook until they are soft (less than 10 minutes). Watch them carefully; they can turn to mush in a flash. Drain the lentils and stir in the brown rice; allow to cool.

Add the turkey, celery, watercress, garlic, green onion, and capers; mix well.

In a 2-cup measure combine the dressing ingredients and blend well. Pour the dressing over the salad and toss lightly, adding more stock if the salad seems dry. Serve on the lettuce leaves, garnish with tomato wedges, and crumble the cheese over the top.

Serves 8.

Turkey and Black Bean Salad

This southwestern-style salad is nourishing and zesty. Serve it with Skinny Corn Bread (page 152) or baked corn tortillas, cut into wedges.

1/2 teaspoon ground cumin
1/2 teaspoon chili powder
Dash salt
Dash cayenne pepper
12 ounces turkey breast cutlets, cut into strips
Vegetable spray, for pan
2 cups tightly packed shredded red leaf lettuce
2 cups tightly packed shredded romaine lettuce
2 oranges, pith removed, each section cut in half
2 stalks celery, with tops, chopped
1 small red bell pepper, chopped
1/2 red onion, chopped
1 can (15 ounces) black beans, rinsed and drained

Lime Dressing
1/4 cup fresh lime juice
2 tablespoons orange juice
2 teaspoons canola oil
1/3 cup chopped cilantro or parsley
1 small clove garlic, minced

In a large zip-top plastic bag, combine the cumin, chili powder, salt, and cayenne. Add the turkey, seal the bag, and shake to coat the turkey with the seasoning mixture.

Coat a large nonstick skillet with cooking spray and place over medium-high heat until hot. Add the seasoned turkey and sauté, stirring, until lightly browned (about 4 minutes). Spoon into a large bowl and add the lettuces, orange sections, celery, bell pepper, onion, and beans. Toss lightly to blend.

In a 4-cup measure whisk together the dressing ingredients. Pour over the salad and toss gently to coat. Serve at room temperature.

Serves 4.

Warm Tuna Salade Provençale

Fresh tuna served warm transforms this classic Mediterranean salad. Serve it with thick slices of whole-grain French bread and chilled medium-dry white wine.

4 medium red potatoes, cut into eighths
1/2 cup tomato juice
4 tablespoons white wine vinegar, divided
2 tablespoons olive oil, divided
1/2 teaspoon salt
1/2 teaspoon freshly ground pepper
1 pound young whole green beans, ends removed, cut in half
12 ounces tuna steak, sliced thin
3 large cloves garlic, minced
1 large red bell pepper, cut into strips
1/2 cup Chicken Stock (page 146)
1/2 teaspoon Herbes de Provence (page 150)
2 teaspoons Dijon mustard
2 tablespoons capers
2 tablespoons freshly squeezed lemon juice
Lettuce leaves, for serving
1 large ripe tomato, cut into thin wedges
Flat-leaf (Italian) parsley sprigs, for garnish

Place the potatoes in a steamer basket over boiling water. Cover and steam until tender (about 10 minutes). Transfer to a large salad bowl, reserving the steaming water. Add the tomato juice, 1 tablespoon of the vinegar, 1 tablespoon of the oil, the salt, and ground pepper and toss gently. Set aside.

Place the green beans in the steamer basket, cover, and steam until crisp-tender (about 5 minutes). Remove the steamer basket and set aside to cool.

In a nonstick skillet over medium-high heat, warm 2 teaspoons of the oil. Add the tuna and sauté until it is opaque (3 to 5 minutes). Spoon the tuna over the potato mixture. Add the remaining 1 teaspoon oil to the skillet with the garlic and bell pepper and sauté, stirring, until they are lightly browned.

Add the remaining 3 tablespoons vinegar, stock, and herb mixture to the skillet. Bring to a boil, stirring, and boil for 2 minutes. Blend in the mustard. Spoon over the potato mixture. Add the cooled green beans, capers, and lemon juice to the potato mixture; toss gently.

To serve, arrange the lettuce leaves (shredded, if you like) on 4 plates. Spoon the warm salad over them. Garnish with the tomato wedges and parsley sprigs.

Serves 4.

Bell Peppers Stuffed with Tuna and Couscous

Here is an adaptation of a traditional Middle Eastern combination. Serve it with whole wheat pita bread.

2 large green bell peppers, halved lengthwise, seeds and membranes removed
1 cup Vegetable Stock (page 147) or water
1 cup couscous
1/2 cup chopped red bell pepper
1/2 cup finely chopped zucchini
1/2 cup chopped flat-leaf (Italian) parsley
1/4 cup chopped red onion
1/4 cup lemon juice
1/2 teaspoon ground allspice
1 tablespoon red wine vinegar
1 tablespoon olive oil
1 can (6 1/2 ounces) chunk tuna in water, drained and flaked
4 Boston lettuce leaves, for serving
2 tablespoons sesame seeds, toasted

Arrange the bell pepper halves cut side down on a rack over boiling water. Cover and steam until crisp-tender (about 8 minutes). Plunge into cold water, then drain on a clean tea towel.

In a medium saucepan over high heat, bring the stock to a boil. Stir in the couscous and boil for 1 minute; then remove from the heat, cover, and let stand for 5 minutes.

Fluff the couscous with a fork and spoon it into a large bowl. Add the bell pepper, zucchini, parsley, and onion; toss lightly.

In a 2-cup measure combine the lemon juice, allspice, vinegar, and oil; whisk to combine. Add to the salad and toss well. Add the tuna and toss again.

To serve, spoon the salad into the drained pepper halves and place them on the lettuce leaves. Sprinkle with the sesame seeds.

Serves 4.

Beet and Herring Salad

This recipe comes from Finland, although variations of it are served all over northern Europe. The Finns would serve it with whole-grain flatbread (available boxed in the supermarket) or rye crisp. Accompany the salad with cold beer. Note that the salad must be refrigerated for several hours or overnight.

2 cups diced cooked potato
1 cup diced cooked carrot
1 1/2 cups diced cooked beet, juice reserved for the dressing
2 tablespoons minced onion
3/4 cup pickled herring, drained and cut into small pieces
1 dill pickle, chopped
1 tart red-skinned apple, unpeeled and diced
Lettuce leaves, for serving
Parsley sprigs, for garnish

Dressing
1/2 cup plain nonfat yogurt
1 1/2 teaspoons lemon juice
1 teaspoon beet juice
Dash sugar
Dash salt
Dash freshly ground black pepper

In a large bowl combine the potato, carrot, beet, onion, herring, pickle, and apple. In a 2-cup measure mix the dressing ingredients and add them to the salad. Blend well, cover, and refrigerate for several hours or overnight.

To serve, spoon the salad onto the lettuce leaves and garnish with the parsley.

Serves 4 to 6.

Warm Fresh Salmon Salad

Although I am not a great practitioner of *la belle présentation*, this dish would win a prize for beauty and elegance. It has unusual ingredients, all of which are available in well-stocked supermarkets or specially stores. (Grow your own arugula if you don't already do so; it grows simply and produces abundantly.) Serve the salad with thin slices of fine-grained whole wheat bread and a first-class dry white wine.

4 medium heads Belgian endive
1/2 pound young green beans
1 head (about 1/2 pound) red leaf lettuce, cut into large pieces, *or* 1/2 pound radicchio
5 ounces arugula, cut into 4-inch pieces
1 pound skinless, boneless salmon fillets, cut lengthwise into thirds
2 tablespoons olive oil
Freshly ground black pepper, to taste
1 cup chopped green onion
2 tablespoons chopped shallot
1 tablespoon minced peeled fresh ginger
1/3 cup white wine vinegar, preferably tarragon
2 tablespoons low-sodium soy sauce
2 tablespoons dry white wine
6 tablespoons chopped fresh dill weed *or* 2 table-spoons dried dill weed
6 lemon wedges

Trim the hard bottoms from the endive and remove the leaves (save the bottoms for another salad). Arrange 8 leaves on each of 6 plates, with the bottoms at the center and the tops forming a fan. Leave room between each leaf.

Lightly steam the green beans; allow to cool. Distribute the red leaf lettuce between the endive leaves and arrange the beans on top of the lettuce. Place a clump of arugula at the center of the fan.

Cut each piece of salmon diagonally into 2-inch-long strips. In a large nonstick skillet over medium heat, warm the oil. Add the salmon strips and grind the pepper over the pieces. Sauté, stirring, for 1 to 2 minutes. Add the green onion, shallot, and fresh ginger. Continue to sauté until the salmon flakes with a fork. Add the vinegar and soy sauce and stir to blend; then stir in the wine and mix well. Remove from the heat.

To serve, place the salmon strips over the salad greens and evenly distribute the sauce over both salmon and greens. Garnish each plate with the chopped dill and 1 lemon wedge.

Serves 6.

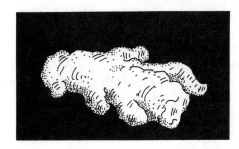

Shrimp with Lime Dressing

Once you have prepared the shrimp, this meal is easy. Serve the salad with warm flour tortillas and chilled beer.

1 lime, halved
1/2 teaspoon coarsely ground black pepper
1/4 teaspoon allspice berries
2 large bay leaves
4 cups water
12 ounces unshelled shrimp
1 small red onion, minced
1 medium ripe tomato, diced
5 radishes, sliced very thin
1/2 green bell pepper, chopped
1 1/2 tablespoons finely chopped cilantro
3 tablespoons lime juice
2 tablespoons olive oil
1/2 teaspoon salt
4 leaves romaine or leaf lettuce, for serving
Cilantro sprigs, for garnish

Squeeze the lime halves into a large saucepan, then add the squeezed rinds, ground pepper, allspice, bay leaves, and the water. Crush the allspice berries against the side of the pan. Cover and bring to a boil; then reduce the heat and simmer for 10 minutes.

Increase the heat to high and add the shrimp. Cover and let the mixture return to a full boil. Immediately remove the pan from the heat and drain off all the liquid. Cover tightly and set aside for 15 minutes.

Meanwhile, in a large bowl combine the onion, tomato, radishes, bell pepper, and cilantro; set aside. In a 1-cup measure combine the lime juice, oil, and salt; set aside.

Rinse the cooked shrimp under cold water, peel, and devein. If the shrimp are medium or larger, cut them into 1/2-inch pieces. Add the shrimp to the vegetables.

Just before serving, stir the lime mixture well and pour over the salad. Toss thoroughly.

To serve, line a platter or shallow bowl with the lettuce leaves. Spoon the salad on top and garnish with the cilantro sprigs.

Serves 4.

Cucumber and Soybean Salad

This Middle Eastern combination makes a nourishing yet refreshing meal and looks very colorful on a bed of greens. Consult the Appendix for cooking the soybeans and lentils (red lentils take only 10 minutes to cook). Serve the salad with warm pita bread.

2 cups cooked soybeans
1 cup cooked red lentils
1 large green bell pepper, chopped
1 medium cucumber, chopped
1/2 cup chopped celery
1/2 cup chopped green onion
1 large clove garlic, crushed in a garlic press
2 tablespoons chopped parsley
2 tablespoons olive oil
2 tablespoons Tomato Puree (page 148)
1/4 cup red wine vinegar
1/4 cup Vegetable Stock (page 147)
1 teaspoon honey
1 teaspoon Worcestershire sauce
1 teaspoon celery seeds
1/4 teaspoon mild paprika
1/4 teaspoon ground allspice
1/4 teaspoon salt
1/4 cup nonfat dry milk
1 cup plain nonfat yogurt
Lettuce leaves, for serving

Place the soybeans and lentils in a large salad bowl. Add the bell pepper, cucumber, celery, green onion, garlic, and parsley; mix thoroughly.

In a 4-cup measure combine the oil, Tomato Puree, vinegar, stock, honey, Worcestershire sauce, celery seeds, paprika, allspice, and salt. Blend well, then pour over the bean mixture and toss gently. Refrigerate for at least 1 hour.

Just before serving, whisk the powdered milk into the yogurt. Stir into the salad. Spoon the salad onto the lettuce leaves and serve.

Serves 6.

Variation

Black-eyed Pea and Vegetable Salad. Substitute 2 cups cooked black-eyed peas for the soybeans and 1/2 teaspoon dry mustard for the allspice. Omit the honey and Worcestershire sauce.

Warm Lentil and Red Bell Pepper Salad

This salad is also Middle Eastern in origin, with the lentils and rice combination that is widely consumed in that region. Serve with whole wheat pita, split and cut into triangles, baked or broiled until golden.

3/4 cup lentils, rinsed and picked over
1 bay leaf
1/2 teaspoon dried thyme
1 1/2 cups cooked brown rice
1 large red bell pepper, cut into thin strips
2 stalks celery, with tops, chopped
2 carrots, chopped
2 green onions, minced
2 tablespoons minced parsley
Lettuce leaves, for serving
1/2 cup crumbled goat cheese

Dressing

2 tablespoons red wine vinegar
2 tablespoons olive oil
2 tablespoons Vegetable Stock (page 147)
1 teaspoon Dijon mustard
2 cloves garlic, minced
1/2 teaspoon salt
1/2 teaspoon freshly ground black pepper

Place the lentils in a large saucepan, add boiling water to cover, cover the pot, and let stand for 15 minutes. Drain. Cover the lentils with 4 cups fresh water and add the bay leaf and thyme. Bring to a boil, then reduce the heat to low and simmer, uncovered, until tender (about 15 minutes).

Drain the lentils, then place them in a large serving bowl with the rice, stirring to mix. Discard the bay leaf. Keep warm.

Meanwhile, in a 2-cup measure, combine the dressing ingredients and whisk to blend.

To the warm lentils and rice, add the bell pepper, celery, carrots, green onions, and parsley. Stir in the dressing and toss to blend.

To serve, spoon the salad onto the lettuce leaves, then sprinkle with the crumbled cheese.

Serves 6.

Warm Cole Slaw with Sherry

This popular salad has Western European roots but was known in the States before the end of the eighteenth century. The version here adds the extra nourishment and chewiness of whole grains and apples, and parts company with the usual creamy mayonnaise dressing. Serve the salad with hearty whole-grain bread and medium-dry white wine.

1/2 head cabbage (about 1 pound), cored and cut into wedges
2 stalks celery, strings removed, tops reserved, cut into pieces
1 medium carrot, cut into pieces
4 green onions, with tops
2 small to medium red-skinned apples, quartered
2 tablespoons canola oil
1 cup cooked soft wheat berries
Lettuce leaves, for serving
1/4 cup shredded reduced-fat Jarlsberg cheese

Dressing
1 tablespoon canola oil
1 tablespoon white wine vinegar
2 teaspoons coarse-grained mustard
1 teaspoon low-sodium soy sauce
1/4 cup dry sherry
1/4 cup plain nonfat yogurt

With the slicing disk of a food processor, slice the cabbage in as many batches as necessary. Set aside in a large bowl. Slice the celery stalks and add to the cabbage.

With the metal blade of the food processor, coarsely chop the celery tops, carrot pieces, green onions, and apples. Add to the cabbage.

In a large nonstick skillet over medium heat, warm the oil. Carefully add the sliced and chopped vegetables; sauté for 5 minutes, stirring. Return the vegetables to the bowl and stir in the wheat berries, mixing well. Set aside.

To prepare the dressing, reduce the heat to medium-low and add the oil, vinegar, mustard, soy sauce, and sherry. Cook, stirring, until heated through (2 to 3 minutes). Remove from the heat, stir in the yogurt until well blended, and pour over the salad. Toss well to blend.

To serve, mound the salad onto the lettuce leaves and sprinkle with the shredded cheese.

Serves 6.

Mexican Potato Salad

This colorful mixed vegetable salad has a lively flavor. Serve it with Skinny Corn Bread (page 152) and chilled beer.

3 medium red potatoes, cooked and cubed
1 medium tomato, cut in half crosswise, then into
  wedges
1/4 cup diced red bell pepper
1/4 cup cooked corn kernels, cut from the cob
1 stalk celery, diced
2 tablespoons diced red onion
4 pitted black olives, sliced
1 teaspoon minced seeded jalapeño pepper
1/4 cup Marinade for Vegetables (page 150)
1 teaspoon chili powder
Romaine lettuce leaves, for serving

In a salad bowl combine the potatoes, tomato, bell pepper, corn, celery, onion, olives, and jalapeño pepper. Combine the marinade and chili powder and pour over the vegetables. Toss to coat. Cover and refrigerate for at least 2 hours.

Just before serving, toss the salad again, then mound it on the lettuce leaves.

Serves 4.

Basmati Rice Salad

The unique flavor of this rice permeates the salad, which is eaten at room temperature. Serve it with thick slices of whole wheat bread.

1 teaspoon canola oil
1 large onion, chopped fine
1 bay leaf
1 large carrot, julienned
2 cups shredded Swiss chard
2 tablespoons raisins
3 green onions, julienned
1/4 cup lemon juice
1/4 teaspoon freshly grated nutmeg
2 cups cooked basmati rice
1 tablespoon crumbled goat cheese

In a large nonstick skillet over medium heat, warm the oil. Sauté the onion and bay leaf for 5 minutes. Add the carrot and continue to cook until the onion is dark and fragrant and the carrot has softened (about 5 minutes).

Reduce the heat and stir in the Swiss chard, raisins, green onions, lemon juice, and nutmeg. Continue to cook, stirring, until the chard has wilted (about 3 minutes). Stir in the rice.

Remove the pan from the heat and discard the bay leaf. Stir in the cheese. Allow to cool to room temperature before serving.

Serves 4.

Cold Marinated Vegetable Salad

You can vary this mixed vegetable combination to suit your tastes and available ingredients. Serve it with thick slices of whole-grain bread and light red wine.

1 cup small broccoli pieces
1 cup thinly sliced carrot
1 red bell pepper, sliced into thin strips
1 yellow or green bell pepper, sliced into thin strips
1 can (15 ounces) chick-peas, rinsed and drained
2 medium zucchini, quartered lengthwise, then sliced
1 bulb fresh fennel, sliced thin
3 stalks celery, sliced, with tops chopped
3/4 cup Marinade for Vegetables (page 152)
1/4 cup minced fresh basil
Lettuce leaves, for serving

Lightly steam the broccoli pieces and sliced carrot. Allow to cool.

In a large bowl combine the bell peppers, chick-peas, zucchini, fennel, celery, and cooled broccoli and carrot. Mix the marinade and basil together and pour over the vegetables. Toss to mix well. Cover and refrigerate for 2 hours.

Remove the salad from the refrigerator about 30 minutes before serving. Mound it on the lettuce leaves and serve.

Serves 6.

Variations

Tuna and Mixed Vegetable Salad. Omit the fennel and carrot; substitute 2 tomatoes, chopped, and 1 can (6 1/2 ounces) chunk tuna in water, drained and flaked. In place of the fresh basil, stir 1 teaspoon Fines Herbes (page 151) and 1/4 teaspoon dried dill weed into the marinade. Serves 8.

Salade Provençale. Omit the fennel, broccoli, and carrot; substitute 2 tomatoes, chopped; 1/4 cup ripe olives, sliced; and 1 can (6 1/2 ounces) chunk tuna in water, drained and flaked. In place of the fresh basil, stir 1 teaspoon Herbes de Provence (page 150) into the marinade. Serves 6.

Mixed Vegetable Salad. Omit the fennel; substitute 1 cup sliced cooked beets, 1 cup diced cooked potato, and 1 cup lightly cooked cut green beans. In place of the basil, mix 1/2 teaspoon Italian Herb Blend (page 150) or Herb and Pepper Mix (page 151) with the marinade. Serves 8.

Vegetable Nut Rice Salad

This lovely combination of colors and textures is fresh tasting and easily made. Serve it with home-made whole-grain bread and hearty red wine.

1 cup thinly sliced carrot
1 cup chopped red and green bell peppers
1 cup fresh sugar snap peas, cut in half
1 cup sliced fresh mushrooms
1/4 cup minced parsley
2 tablespoons snipped chives
3 cups cooked brown rice
1 cup chopped almonds, toasted
Romaine lettuce leaves, for serving

Dressing
3/4 cup thin tomato juice
1/4 cup red wine vinegar
1 tablespoon chopped green onion
1 clove garlic, crushed
1 teaspoon Herb and Pepper Mix (page 151)

Steam the carrot and peppers until crisp-tender. Rinse in cold water and drain. Steam the peas for less than 1 minute. Rinse and drain. Combine the steamed vegetables with the mushrooms, parsley, chives, rice, and almonds.

Measure the dressing ingredients into a 2-cup measure and whisk until blended. Pour 3/4 cup dressing over the salad (reserve the remainder, refrigerated, for another use) and toss gently.

To serve, mound the salad on the lettuce leaves.

Serves 4 to 6.

Spinach Salad with Spirals

Here is a colorful combination of pasta and fresh vegetables. Try to use vegetable spirals in different colors if possible. Serve with thick slices of crusty Italian bread or Simple Garlic Bread (page 152), and chilled beer.

1/2 cup Slim Yogurt Dressing (page 149)
1/2 teaspoon Italian Herb Blend (page 150)
1 small clove garlic, minced
2 1/2 cups cooked spirals, rinsed and drained
2 cups shredded spinach
1/2 cup finely sliced green onion
1/2 cup finely chopped red bell pepper
2 cups cherry tomatoes or small tomato wedges
1 tablespoon lemon juice
Lettuce leaves, for serving
Freshly grated Parmesan cheese, for garnish

In a 1-cup measure combine the dressing with the herb blend and garlic. Let stand while preparing the salad.

In a large bowl combine the pasta, spinach, green onion, bell pepper, and tomatoes. Stir in the lemon juice.

Pour the dressing over the salad and toss well to combine. Serve at room temperature over the lettuce leaves. Sprinkle lightly with the grated cheese.

Serves 4.

Lentil and Onion Burritos

Burritos are one of several Mexican dishes that resemble a sandwich. A wheat tortilla is filled and rolled. Fillings are spicy and can be meat and poultry or vegetables and legumes, with cheese. A Mexican-American staple, they are generally served with salsa and chilled beer.

Vegetable spray, for pan
2 medium onions, minced
1 teaspoon dried oregano
1/2 teaspoon chili powder
1/2 teaspoon paprika
1/2 teaspoon Hot Pepper Sauce (page 148)
1/4 teaspoon ground cumin
2 cups cooked lentils
4 flour tortillas
1/4 cup shredded reduced-fat Monterey jack
  cheese
1 tablespoon canola oil
4 ripe tomatoes, quartered
1 tablespoon lime juice
Dick's Salsa (page 149)

Coat a large nonstick skillet with vegetable spray. Add the onions, oregano, chili powder, paprika, Hot Pepper Sauce, and cumin. Sauté over medium heat until the mixture is fragrant and the onion is cooked. Mix in the lentils.

Divide the mixture among the tortillas. Sprinkle with the cheese and roll up the tortillas.

Wipe out the skillet. Add the oil and warm over medium-high heat. Add the burritos, seam side down, and heat until the bottoms are just brown (about 2 minutes).

In a food processor puree the tomatoes and lime juice. Flip the burritos over and cover with the tomato mixture. Cover the pan and simmer until the tomatoes are heated through. Serve with the salsa on the side.

Serves 2.

Black Bean Burritos

This method for burritos makes a quick and zesty meal. Serve it with a mixed green salad and chilled beer.

1 tablespoon vegetable oil, or more as needed
2 teaspoons chili powder
1 teaspoon dried oregano
1/4 teaspoon ground cumin
1/2 cup chopped onion
1/2 cup chopped green bell pepper
1 large clove garlic, minced
1 can (15 ounces) black beans, rinsed, drained,
  and mashed
1 can (4 ounces) chopped green chiles, drained
8 flour tortillas
1 cup shredded reduced-fat Monterey jack cheese
Dick's Salsa (page 149)

In a nonstick skillet, over medium heat, warm the oil. Stir in the chili powder, oregano, and cumin and sizzle for several minutes. Add the onion, bell pepper, and garlic and sauté, stirring, until the onion is tender (about 5 minutes). Stir in the beans and chiles.

Spread 1/4 cup of the bean mixture down the center of each tortilla and top each with 2 tablespoons cheese. Roll up. Wipe out the pan, add a little more oil, and heat the tortillas until they are browned on the bottom and the cheese has melted. Serve with the salsa on the side.

Serves 4.

Vegetable and Bean Tostadas

This Mexican-style sandwich is a lot of fun to make. First comes the tortilla, then the sauce, then cheese, then lettuce, tomato, and sunflower seeds. This makes a hearty meal with a glass of chilled beer.

Spicy Vegetable Filling
1 tablespoon canola oil
1 large onion, chopped
2 large carrots, sliced thin
1 clove garlic, minced
2 teaspoons chili powder
3/4 teaspoon ground cumin
3/4 teaspoon dried oregano
4 medium zucchini, cut into 1/2-inch cubes
1 large green bell pepper, chopped
1 cup fresh or frozen corn kernels
1 can (15 ounces) red kidney beans, drained, rinsed, and slightly mashed

Tostadas
10 to 12 corn or flour tortillas (6-inch size)
2 cups shredded reduced-fat Monterey jack or Cheddar cheese
3 cups shredded romaine lettuce leaves
1 large tomato, chopped
1 cup sunflower seeds, toasted
Dick's Salsa (page 149) *or* **Green Chile Salsa (page 149)** *or* **bottled red or green taco sauce**

To prepare the filling, in a large skillet over medium heat, warm the oil. Add the onion, carrots, garlic, chili powder, cumin, and oregano; sauté until the onion is soft. Stir in the zucchini, bell pepper, corn, and mashed beans. Cook, stirring, until the zucchini is tender-crisp (about 5 minutes). Keep warm.

Heat the tortillas in a moderate oven until nearly crisp. To serve, pile the hot filling on top of each tortilla and sprinkle generously with the shredded cheese; then add the shredded lettuce, chopped tomato, and toasted seeds. Serve the salsa on the side. *Serves 10 or more.*

Variation
Turkey and Vegetable Tostadas. To the filling add 1 cup finely chopped cooked turkey (with the zucchini) or 8 ounces fresh ground turkey (cooked with the onion). Serves 12.

Pita Pockets with Bean Filling

This Mexican-style filling for pita bread sandwiches is quickly made. Serve with cold beer.

1 can (15 ounces) pinto beans or black beans, rinsed and drained
1/4 cup Dick's Salsa (page 149) *or* **Green Chile Salsa (page 149)**
1/4 cup diced green bell pepper
2 green onions, minced
1 clove garlic, minced
1 teaspoon lemon juice
1 1/2 cups shredded romaine lettuce leaves
Chopped tomato, for garnish
Sliced cucumber, for garnish
4 whole wheat pita pockets
4 tablespoons shredded reduced-fat Monterey jack cheese

Mash the beans and stir in the salsa, bell pepper, green onions, garlic, and lemon juice. Mix to a fairly smooth consistency. Arrange some of the shredded lettuce, chopped tomato, and cucumber slices in each pita and spoon in the filling. Top each with 1 tablespoon cheese.

Serves 4.

 Appendix

Microwave Uses and Techniques

Although almost none of the recipes in this book call for a microwave oven, I find this appliance to be a real help in some specialized ways, a few of which are discussed here.

The microwave can save you preparation time in the kitchen. If you want to quickly combine a sauce—a smooth, lump-free cream sauce, a tomato sauce, a sauce for the stir-fry, the marinade for a vegetable salad—the microwave is unexcelled. You will find that many of the basic recipes given later in this chapter have a microwave version.

The microwave can shorten the time for soaking legumes (dried beans), although it is not much help in cooking them. You will find it an aid in beating up cooked foods or in defrosting stock and frozen vegetables, for example. Consult the stove manual for times and techniques.

Vegetables cooked in the microwave are simply wonderful, so if a recipe calls for cooked vegetables, think of this quick possibility. Those vegetables that take a long time to cook can be done very quickly; for example, a half pound of small beets can be cooked in about 8 minutes in the microwave. Many vegetables come out perfectly crisp-tender if microwaved properly.

When making a marinated vegetable salad, use the microwave to cook the vegetables. Remember that foods keep on cooking after you have taken them out of the oven, so you may want to rinse them under cold water to stop the cooking process. Pat them dry so that you don't dilute the marinade or dressing, and so that the coating will stick to the vegetables. Chill or leave the vegetables at room temperature until serving time. The vegetables will look colorful and taste very fresh.

If you are making a salad with many different vegetables, you can cook them together. You will need to experiment with times to get the vegetables to the doneness you like. Cook the most dense types—carrots, green beans, onions, broccoli stems, for example—first. Cut them into uniform pieces and microwave for 2 to 3 minutes on high (100%). Then add the quicker-cooking vegetables—broccoli and cauliflower florets, celery, fresh asparagus—and cook them for another 2 minutes.

Lastly, add the really quick-cooking vegetables—sugar snap peas, snow peas, mushrooms, zucchini, yellow summer squash, tomatoes, green onions—and cook them very briefly, no more than a minute.

The microwave is also handy for cooking bacon. The timing depends on the thickness, the number of slices, and the crispness desired. It also depends on the size of the microwave. Two slices cooked crisp usually takes about 3 minutes. Cook the bacon on a double thickness of paper towels with another paper towel for a cover. Consult the stove manual for details.

Timetables and Instructions for Grains and Legumes

Many types of grains and legumes appear often in this book, and for good reason. They are a marvelous source of vitamins, minerals, and fiber. Various grains and legumes are briefly described in the Introduction, but here are some general indications about cooking them.

Grains

The general rule for cooking grains is 2 parts water or stock to 1 part grain. Roughly speaking, 1 cup of dry grain yields about 3 cups cooked. Short-grain rice yields less than that, between 2 and 2 1/2 cups cooked grain, except if you make a risotto and add extra liquid over a period of time. (For a description of cooking risotto, see page 70.)

Cooking times vary from grain to grain, from climate to climate, from one stove to another. Please do not be overly upset if your grain does not cook exactly as I have indicated here. This is the fault of neither of us, but rather of conditions beyond our control. To shorten cooking times considerably, you can soak grains overnight in water to cover.

There are two basic techniques for cooking grain. You can sauté it in a small amount of oil with chopped onion (green or regular) and herbs. Stir frequently and cook until the grain browns somewhat. Then stir in the stock, make sure that it comes to a boil, then reduce the heat, cover, and cook for the desired length of time.

The other technique is to bring the water to a boil, add seasonings and the dry grain, stir, reduce the heat, cover, and simmer for the desired length of time. In both cases you can turn off the heat before all the liquid is absorbed and the grain will continue cooking. This is particularly true if you have an electric stove. Just leave the pan on the burner, covered, until you're ready to serve the grain.

Legumes

Modern research suggests that the amount of carbohydrates that cause intestinal gas can be greatly reduced by soaking legumes overnight and then discarding the water before cooking. Or you can pour boiling water to cover the legumes and soak for 6 hours or so, then discard the water.

I am not totally convinced about this theory and often wonder about the nutrients that go down the drain with the soaking liquid. In most recipes here, however, I do recommend presoaking the legumes and cooking them in fresh water. It does decrease cooking time considerably. The times given here are for presoaked legumes. The yield is generally 3 cups cooked legumes for 1 cup dried. Determining the amount of liquid used is simple: Place the legumes in the pot with enough water to cover by at least 2 inches, adding more water if necessary during cooking. Black-eyed peas, split peas, and lentils need no soaking.

If you cook legumes in a pressure cooker (times are given below), you do not need to soak them. To cook 1 cup legumes, bring 4 cups water to a boil, add the legumes, cover, and bring to 15 pounds pressure. Cook according to the times given below. Cool the pressure cooker under cold running water, open, and drain the liquid from the cooked legumes.

Grain Cooking Chart

Grain (1 cup)	Liquid (cups)	Cooking Time (minutes)	Yield (cups)
Rice, long-grain			
White	2	15 to 20	3
Brown	2 1/2	45 to 50	3
Brown aromatics	2-2 1/2	40 to 45	3 1/2
Rice, short-grain			
White	2	15	2
Brown	3	50	2 1/4
Barley			
Pearl	3	35 to 40	3 to 4
Pearl	(presoaked in 2 cups water)	15	3 to 4
Hulled	(presoaked in 4 1/2 cups water)	60	3
Bulgur*	2 1/2	20	3
Millet*	2 1/2	20	3
Couscous *(see page 93)*			
Wheat berries (presoaked in 3 1/2 cups water)		60	2
Wild rice	3	50 to 60	3 to 4

*Allow the grains to stand, covered, for 10 minutes after they have finished cooking. Millet is greatly improved in taste if you brown it first (dry, no fat in the pan) for about 5 minutes before cooking.

Legume Cooking Chart

Legumes	Regular Cooking	Pressure Cooking
Black beans, kidney beans, pinto beans	2 hours	20-25 minutes
Soy beans	2 1/2 hours	30 minutes
Red beans (adzuki)	3 hours	30-35 minutes
Chick-peas (garbanzos)	3 hours	30-35 minutes
Black-eyed peas, split peas, lentils	1 hour	10-15 minutes
Red lentils	10 minutes	

Basic Recipes

Stocks

The secret of good stock is fresh ingredients and sufficient cooking time. Try to make a considerable amount of stock at one time. Chill all stock before you use it and remove any fat that has risen to the top.

Homemade stock is perishable, although beef and vegetable stock will keep longer (up to a week) in the refrigerator than chicken and turkey stock (2 to 3 days).

If you want to keep the stock longer, store it in the freezer, where it will keep for at least 6 months. For safety's sake, before using stock—whether refrigerated or frozen—bring it to a full boil.

If you use canned stock, either as a supplement or as an ingredient in a recipe, remember that it is salted, so season accordingly.

Beef Stock

Remove all visible fat from 4 pounds raw beef bones, including some veal bones if you can get them, and some meat (include a piece or two of shin bone, if you like). Brown them in a wide soup pot over medium-high heat, or bake them, uncovered, in a 450 degree F oven until brown (about 30 minutes), turning once. Add 3 large onions, chopped, and brown them for part of the time. Let the pot cool somewhat and add 14 cups water, scraping the bottom of the pot to deglaze. Then add 4 medium carrots, coarsely chopped; 4 stalks celery, with tops, chopped; 3 cloves garlic, cut into pieces; 6 sprigs parsley; 2 bay leaves; 10 peppercorns; 2 teaspoons salt; and 2 tablespoons red wine vinegar. Bring the stock to a boil; then reduce the heat to low and simmer, partially covered, for 3 hours. Stir in 2 tablespoons red wine vinegar and continue to simmer, partially covered, until the liquid is reduced to about 2 quarts. Strain. Use the meat and vegetables for soup, if you like. Makes 2 quarts.

Remember that if you make Pot au Feu (page 97), you will have some stock already made.

Chicken Stock

If you have a chicken carcass from a roast, brown the bones in a wide stockpot over medium-high heat. Otherwise, boil 4 pounds chicken pieces (backs, necks, and wings) in 4 quarts water. Skim, then add 2 medium onions, quartered; 2 cloves garlic, quartered; 2 medium carrots, chopped; 2 stalks celery, with tops, chopped; 8 sprigs parsley; 10 peppercorns; 1 teaspoon salt; 1 teaspoon fresh thyme (or 1/2 teaspoon dried thyme); 1 tablespoon cider vinegar; and enough water to cover the chicken by 3 inches. Return to a boil; then reduce the heat to low and simmer, partially covered, skimming occasionally, until the stock is reduced to 3 quarts (about 3 hours). Strain. Makes 3 quarts.

Turkey Stock

I always save the carcass from the holiday roast turkey to make stock. Otherwise, you can use 4 pounds turkey pieces (backs, necks, and wings). In either case, follow the directions above for Chicken Stock, adding 1 teaspoon rubbed dried sage and 1/2 teaspoon dried rosemary to the stock.

Fish Stock

In a large stockpot combine 2 1/2 pounds heads and bones of firm-fleshed white fish, cleaned of blood and cut into 2-inch pieces, with 6 cups water and 1 cup dry white wine. Add 2 medium onions, chopped; 2 medium stalks celery, with tops, chopped; 6 sprigs parsley; 1 bay leaf; 8 peppercorns; 1 teaspoon salt; and the juice of 1 lemon. Bring to a boil, then reduce the heat to medium-low and simmer, partially covered, for about 1 hour. Strain. Makes 1 1/2 to 2 quarts. If you like, add 3 cups clam juice to the stock with the other ingredients.

Microwave version. Use 2 pounds fish heads and bones, 1 onion, 1 celery stalk, 1 carrot cut into 1-inch lengths, the seasonings given above, and 5 cups liquid. Place everything in a 2-quart soufflé dish, cover tightly with microwave plastic wrap, and cook on high (100%) for 20 minutes. Remove from the microwave and leave covered until the bubbling stops (about 3 minutes). Uncover carefully and strain.

Vegetable Stock

In a large stockpot combine 2 cloves garlic, cut; 5 medium onions, chopped; 4 stalks celery, with leaves, coarsely chopped; 1 bunch parsley; 1 teaspoon fresh lemon thyme *or* 1/2 teaspoon dried thyme; 1/4 teaspoon crumbled dried sage; 1 bay leaf; 1 teaspoon salt; 10 peppercorns, lightly crushed; 5 allspice berries, lightly crushed; and 4 quarts water. Bring to a boil; then reduce the heat to low and simmer, partially covered, until the liquid is reduced to about 2 1/2 quarts (about 2 hours). Stir in 1 tablespoon red wine vinegar and continue to simmer, uncovered, for 30 minutes longer. Strain, gently pressing the liquid out of the vegetables with the back of a spoon. Makes about 2 1/2 quarts.

To make Vegetable Stock with tomatoes, add 2 medium tomatoes, coarsely chopped, to the pot with the other vegetables.

Microwave variation. Combine the above ingredients, using only 3 quarts water, in a 5-quart casserole. Cover tightly with microwave plastic wrap and cook on high (100%) for 35 minutes. Prick the plastic wrap to release the steam; then remove from the oven and allow the stock to stop bubbling. Remove the cover. Strain, pressing to extract all the stock.

Root Vegetable Stock

In a wide stockpot over medium heat, warm 1 tablespoon canola oil. Stir in 3 large carrots, chopped; 1 large turnip, chopped; 2 large stalks celery, with tops, coarsely chopped; 2 large onions, chopped; and 2 cloves garlic, quartered. Sauté the vegetables, stirring occasionally, until golden (about 15 minutes). Carefully pour in 3 quarts water, stir well, and add 1 teaspoon salt, 6 large sprigs parsley, 1 bay leaf, 1 teaspoon dried thyme, and 6 black peppercorns.

Bring to a boil; then reduce the heat and simmer, partially covered, for about 2 hours. Strain, pressing on the strainer to extract all the liquid, and discard the vegetables. Makes about 10 cups.

Tomato Sauce

In a large saucepan over medium heat, warm 1 tablespoon olive oil. Add 1 large onion, chopped; 1/2 green bell pepper, seeded and chopped; 2 stalks celery, with tops, chopped; 2 carrots, cut into pieces; and 1 large clove garlic, chopped. Sauté the vegetables for about 5 minutes. Then stir in 6 large tomatoes, quartered (or 4 cups canned tomatoes—reserve the juice for another use), 1 bay leaf, 1 teaspoon brown sugar, 3 sprigs parsley, 1 teaspoon dried basil, 1 teaspoon salt, and 1/4 teaspoon freshly ground black pepper. Reduce the heat to low and gently cook the sauce until thick (about 45 minutes), stirring occasionally. If the tomatoes are watery, drain off some of the juice and reserve for another use; it makes a lovely base for salad dressings or as a light vegetable stock for cooking rice or meat loaf. Discard the bay leaf and puree the sauce in the food processor. Makes about 4 cups.

Marinara Sauce

In a large saucepan over medium heat, warm 1 tablespoon olive oil. Sauté 1 large onion, chopped; 1/2 large green bell pepper, chopped; and 2 cloves garlic, chopped, until lightly browned. Stir in 1 can (28 ounces) whole tomatoes or Italian plum tomatoes (drain off the juice and reserve for another use); 1 can (6 ounces) tomato paste; 1/4 cup minced parsley, preferably flat-leaf (Italian); 1 tablespoon Italian Herb Blend (page 150); 1/2 teaspoon salt; and 1/2 teaspoon freshly ground black pepper. Cook, uncovered, for about 45 minutes, stirring occasionally. Makes about 3 cups.

Variation. If desired, add 1 small zucchini, quartered, then sliced, and/or 1/4 pound fresh mushrooms, sliced, with the tomatoes and tomato paste.

You can also add 2 tablespoons dry red wine for a more robust flavor.

Microwave version. Place the onion, bell pepper, and garlic in a food processor and process until finely chopped. Heat the oil in a 2-quart soufflé dish, uncovered, on high (100%) for 1 minute. Stir in the chopped vegetables. Cook, uncovered, on high for 8 minutes, stirring once. Stir in the remaining ingredients and cook on high for 8 minutes. Taste and adjust the seasonings.

Spaghetti Sauce

In a large nonstick skillet over medium heat, sauté about 1/2 pound lean ground beef and 3 ounces mild or hot Italian turkey sausage (skinned and cut into small pieces), stirring to break up the meat, until the meat and sausage are lightly browned. Drain off any excess fat. Stir in 3 cups of either the Tomato Sauce or the Marinara Sauce above, according to your taste. Makes about 4 cups.

Crushed Tomatoes

This is a quickly made microwave concentrate for use in sauces and soups or as a salad dressing base. Freeze it in 1-cup and 2-cup portions and also in an ice cube tray to add quick tomato flavor to a dish.

Remove the core and cut a deep X across the bottom of 12 medium tomatoes. Place in a 2 1/2-quart soufflé dish or square baking dish. Cook, uncovered, on high (100%) for 20 minutes, stirring once. Remove from the microwave and pass through a food mill. You should have about 8 cups cooked tomatoes.

Return them to the dish. Cook, uncovered, on high until all the liquid has evaporated (about 45 minutes). Remove from the oven and let cool completely. Store, tightly covered, in the refrigerator, or freeze as indicated above. Makes about 4 cups.

Tomato Puree

Combine 5 pounds plum tomatoes, cored and cut into 1-inch pieces, with 12 cloves garlic, mashed, in a 4-quart saucepan. Stir in 1/4 cup olive oil. Simmer, uncovered, stirring occasionally, until the tomatoes and garlic are soft (about 1 hour). Pass the mixture through a food mill or sieve, discard the pulp, and return the puree to the pan. Simmer, uncovered and stirring often, until the mixture becomes thick (1 to 1 1/2 hours). Cooking time depends considerably on the tomatoes used. Stir in 1/2 teaspoon salt and 1/2 teaspoon freshly ground black pepper. Taste and add more seasoning, if desired. Store, tightly covered, in the refrigerator for up to 1 week or freeze for up to 2 months. Makes 4 cups.

Microwave version. Combine the tomatoes, garlic, and oil in a 5-quart casserole dish with a tight fitting lid. Cover and cook on high (100%) for 15 minutes. While the dish is still in the microwave, uncover and stir, then cover and cook until the tomatoes and garlic are soft (about 10 minutes longer). Puree as above, then return the dish to the oven. Cook, uncovered, on high, stirring occasionally, until the mixture becomes thick (35 to 45 minutes). Season to taste.

Hot Pepper Sauce

In a small saucepan combine 1/4 cup olive oil, 2 1/2 teaspoons cayenne pepper, 1 1/2 teaspoons cumin, 1 clove garlic (crushed in a press), and 1/4 teaspoon salt. Cook until well blended. Serve warm. Good over fish dishes and stews.

Rouille

In a medium saucepan combine 2 small green bell peppers (seeded and cut into pieces), 2 tablespoons chopped red bell pepper, 1 ancho chile, and 1 cup water. Simmer until the peppers are tender (about 10 minutes). Drain thoroughly and dry them with paper towels. Then process them together with 4 garlic cloves and 3 tablespoons olive oil in a food processor until smooth. Transfer the sauce to a bowl and stir in enough fine dried bread crumbs (1 to 3 tablespoons) to make the sauce thick enough to hold its shape in a spoon. If desired, omit the chile and stir a few drops of Tabasco sauce into the finished mixture.

Dick's Salsa

This makes a mild salsa. Feel free to add more chiles to taste. In a food processor combine 1 can (16 ounces) peeled tomatoes (drain and reserve juice for another use); 2 ripe tomatoes; 1/2 large green bell pepper, seeded and cut into pieces; chiles, such as 1/2 jalapeño, 1/4 Hungarian wax, and 1 small piece serrano, seeded and cut into pieces, to taste; 5 green onions; 4 sprigs parsley or cilantro; 1/2 teaspoon ground cumin; and 1/4 teaspoon cayenne pepper. Pulse on and off until the salsa ingredients are chopped but not smooth. Taste and season with salt and freshly ground black pepper.

To make corn salsa, stir in about 1 cup cooked corn cut from the cob and 1 tablespoon lime juice.

Green Chile Salsa

In a food processor combine 1 pound tomatillos, peeled; 2 cloves garlic, quartered; 1 fresh green hot chile, such as jalapeño or serrano, or to taste; 1/4 cup chopped green onion, with tops; and 1/2 cup cilantro leaves. Coarsely puree, then season to taste with salt and stir in 1 teaspoon sugar.

Pesto

Everyone seems to be growing fresh basil these days so they can make this sensational sauce. It will keep well in the refrigerator in an airtight container topped with olive oil to seal. If you freeze it, blend in the pine nuts or cheese just before you use it.

In a food processor combine 4 cups fresh basil leaves; 3 cloves garlic, chopped coarsely; 1/2 cup pine nuts; 1/2 cup flat-leaf (Italian) parsley; 1/4 cup olive oil; and 1/4 teaspoon salt. Blend to a smooth paste. If it is too thick, add a little water. Then add 1/4 cup Parmesan cheese and process again. To use as a sauce over pasta, dilute with 2 tablespoons of the hot pasta water and toss with the cooked pasta.

Slim Yogurt Dressing

I use this mildly flavored salad dressing more often than any other. It is quick and unbelievably easy, and contains no oil. Feel free to vary ingredients to your taste and to add some herbs. In any event allow the dressing to stand for a while to blend flavors. If you find it too thick, dilute with a little buttermilk or vegetable stock.

In a 2-cup measure combine 1 cup plain low-fat yogurt, 2 tablespoons balsamic vinegar, 2 rounded teaspoons coarsely ground mustard, and 1/4 teaspoon garlic granules. That's it. Makes almost 1 1/4 cups.

Creamy Vinaigrette

In a 2-cup measure combine 1/2 cup plain low-fat yogurt, 1/4 cup red wine or sherry vinegar, 1 tablespoon canola oil, 2 teaspoons Dijon mustard, 1 small clove garlic (crushed in garlic press), and a dash freshly ground black pepper. Makes a little more than 3/4 cup.

Light Herb Dressing

Combine 1/2 cup Vegetable Stock (page 147) or thin tomato juice with 1/4 cup red wine vinegar, 1/4 teaspoon Fines Herbes (page 151), 1 small clove garlic (crushed in garlic press), and a dash each of sugar, salt, and freshly ground white pepper. Makes about 3/4 cup.

Sesame Dressing

In a 2-cup measure combine 4 tablespoons water, 2 tablespoons rice vinegar, 2 tablespoons low-sodium soy sauce, 1 tablespoon Asian sesame oil, 1/4 teaspoon Chinese five-spice powder, and 1 tablespoon sesame seeds, toasted. Makes more than 1/2 cup.

Orange Ginger Dressing

In a 2-cup measure combine 1/4 cup fresh orange juice, 1 tablespoon canola oil, 1 tablespoon minced green onion, 1 teaspoon minced peeled fresh ginger, 1/2 teaspoon grated orange zest, and 1/4 teaspoon minced garlic. Stir well and add a little salt and ground pepper to taste. Makes more than 1/3 cup.

Creamy Orange Dressing

In a blender combine 1 cup nonfat cottage cheese, 1/2 cup orange juice, 1 tablespoon honey, 2 teaspoons grated orange zest, 1 teaspoon ground mustard, and a dash salt. Process at high speed until smooth. Makes about 1 cup.

Yogurt Dill Sauce

Combine 1 1/2 cups plain nonfat yogurt, 1 tablespoon Dijon mustard, 1 tablespoon minced fresh chives, 2 teaspoons dried dill weed, and a dash prepared horseradish. Excellent for a fish salad.

Yogurt Herb Topping

Combine 1/2 cup plain low-fat yogurt, 1/2 cup nonfat cottage cheese, 1 teaspoon lemon juice, 1 teaspoon minced fresh chives, and 1 teaspoon Herbes de Provence (this page) or Italian Herb Blend (this page). This makes a delicious topping for baked potatoes or a potato salad or casserole.

Marinade for Vegetables

In a food processor chop 1 onion, 2 shallots, 1/2 carrot, 1/2 celery stalk, with tops, and 1 clove garlic. In a large saucepan heat 1/4 cup olive oil; sauté the chopped vegetables until soft and lightly browned.

Stir in 3/4 cup cider vinegar or white wine vinegar, 2 cups light red wine, 1 bay leaf, 1 teaspoon dried thyme, 1/2 teaspoon ground coriander, 1/2 teaspoon salt, and 1/2 teaspoon freshly ground black pepper. Simmer, uncovered, for about 40 minutes. Discard the bay leaf. Let cool completely. Use as a dressing over warm slightly cooked vegetables. Makes about 3 cups.

Microwave version. In a 2-quart soufflé dish, heat the oil on high (100%) for 1 minute. Add the chopped vegetables and cook, uncovered, on high for 8 minutes, stirring once. Add the remaining ingredients, stir, and cook on high for 10 minutes, stirring once or twice. Let cool and discard the bay leaf.

Yogurt Cheese

Line a strainer or colander with a damp clean cheesecloth about 20 inches square. Pour in 4 cups plain nonfat yogurt. Fold the cloth over and twist the ends to form a pouch. Place the pouch over a large bowl and let it drain at room temperature for 3 to 5 hours, then refrigerate until the next day. Discard the liquid. Unwrap and invert the yogurt cheese onto a serving plate. Store, covered, in the refrigerator. Use in cooking or blend with herbs for a dip or spread.

Italian Herb Blend

You can buy commercial Italian seasoning or you can make your own by combining 3 tablespoons dried oregano, 2 tablespoons dried basil, 1 tablespoon dried marjoram, 1 tablespoon dried thyme, and 2 teaspoons crushed dried rosemary in a 4-cup measure. Blend and crush somewhat with your fingers. Store in an airtight container in a cool, dry, dark place. Makes about 1/2 cup.

Herbes de Provence

Combine the following herbs: 3 tablespoons dried thyme, 3 tablespoons dried marjoram, 2 tablespoons dried summer savory, 1 teaspoon dried rosemary, 1 teaspoon crumbled dried mint, 1/2 teaspoon fennel seeds, 1/4 teaspoon rubbed dried sage, and 1/4 teaspoon dried lavender flowers. Store in a jar with a tight-fitting lid.

Crush with a mortar and pestle before using. Makes about 1/2 cup.

Fines Herbes

This mixture is available commercially but it is easily made. Crush the herbs slightly, and store in an airtight container. Combine 2 tablespoons dried thyme, 2 tablespoons dried oregano, 2 tablespoons dried marjoram, 2 tablespoons dried parsley, 2 tablespoons dried chervil, 1 tablespoon dried chopped chives, 1 teaspoon rubbed dried sage, and 1 teaspoon dried tarragon. Store in a cool, dry, dark place. Makes about 3/4 cup.

Herb and Pepper Mix

This dried herb mixture can be used in place of salt. Combine 1 tablespoon garlic granules, 1/2 teaspoon freshly ground white pepper, 1/2 freshly ground black pepper, and 1/4 teaspoon cayenne pepper with 1 teaspoon of each of the following: rubbed dried sage, dried basil, dried marjoram, dried thyme, dried parsley, dried winter savory, ground mace, and onion powder. Mix gently with your fingers. Store in an airtight container in a cool, dry, dark place. Makes about 1/3 cup.

Cajun Pepper Mix

Combine 2 tablespoons paprika, 4 teaspoons cayenne pepper, 2 teaspoons coarsely ground black pepper, 1 teaspoon dried chives, 1 teaspoon dried basil, 1/2 teaspoon freshly ground white pepper, 1/2 teaspoon crushed red pepper flakes, 1/4 teaspoon onion powder, and 1/4 teaspoon garlic granules. Mix together thoroughly. Store in an airtight container in a cool, dry, dark place. Makes about 1/3 cup.

Cajun Herb and Spice Mix

Heat a small dry skillet over medium-high heat and add 1 teaspoon fennel seeds and 1/4 teaspoon cumin seeds. Cook, stirring constantly and shaking the pan, until lightly browned and fragrant (2 to 3 minutes). Let cool and grind to a fine powder in a blender or spice mill. Then combine with 2 tablespoons onion powder, 2 tablespoons garlic granules, 1 tablespoon paprika, 1 teaspoon freshly ground black pepper, 1 teaspoon freshly ground white pepper, 1 teaspoon dried oregano, 1 teaspoon dried thyme, 1/2 teaspoon red pepper flakes, and 1/4 teaspoon crushed saffron threads. Store in an airtight container in the refrigerator for up to 6 months. Makes about 1/3 cup.

Whole Wheat Pizza Dough

In a large mixing bowl, combine 2 cups fine whole wheat flour, 1 cup all-purpose flour, 1 1/2 ounces fast-acting yeast, 1 teaspoon sugar, and 1/2 teaspoon salt. Stir in 1 cup warm water. If you have a dough hook, mix with your mixer for 15 minutes. If not, turn out onto a floured surface and knead until smooth (about 10 minutes).

Place the dough in a lightly greased bowl, turn to coat, cover with a damp cloth, and let rise in a warm place until doubled in bulk (about 1 hour). Punch down the dough and divide in half. Roll out each half into a 12-inch circle and place on pizza pans that have each been sprinkled with 1/2 tablespoon cornmeal. Crimp the edges of the dough to form a rim.

If you want a soft dough, let it rise again for about 30 minutes. If not, immediately cover with the topping. If you are making only one pizza, store the other half of the dough in the freezer for up to 1 month.

Note: You can add 1 teaspoon Italian Herb Blend (page 150) to the dough, if desired.

Parsley Dumplings

In a medium bowl combine 1 cup all-purpose flour, 2 teaspoons baking powder, 1/4 teaspoon salt, 2 teaspoons canola oil, 3 tablespoons minced parsley, and 1/2 cup skim milk until just moist.

Note: To make cornmeal dumplings, substitute 1/4 cup yellow cornmeal for 1/4 cup of the flour and increase the liquid slightly.

Skinny Corn Bread

In a medium bowl combine 3/4 cup yellow cornmeal, 1/2 cup whole wheat flour, 2 teaspoons baking powder, 1/2 cup baking soda, and 1/4 teaspoon salt. In a 4-cup measure combine 1 beaten egg, 1 tablespoon honey, and 3/4 cup skim milk or buttermilk; pour over the cornmeal mixture, stirring until just moistened. Pour into a lightly oiled 9- by 5-inch bread pan and bake at 400 degrees F for 20 minutes. Let cool slightly, then cut into slices.

If desired, you can add 1/4 cup chopped pecans or 1/4 cup cooked corn kernels to the batter.

Triple Wheat Biscuits

Sift together 1 1/4 cups all-purpose flour, 1/4 cup whole wheat pastry flour, 1/4 teaspoon salt, and 1/4 teaspoon baking soda into a mixing bowl. Stir in 1/2 cup wheat germ. Add 2 tablespoons light margarine and 2 tablespoons farmer cheese or well-drained nonfat cottage cheese and cut in until crumbly. With a fork mix in 3/4 cup buttermilk. Turn out and knead about 6 times. Roll 1/2-inch thick. Cut with a 2-inch cutter and bake on an ungreased baking sheet at 450 degrees F for 8 to 10 minutes. Makes 1 dozen.

Simple Garlic Bread

Mix together 2 tablespoons olive oil, 1 large clove garlic (crushed in a garlic press), 1 teaspoon Italian Herb Blend (page 150), and a pinch salt. You can also add some minced fresh herbs, if you wish. Cut about 1/2 loaf whole-grain French bread or Italian bread into thick slices almost to the bottom.

With a pastry brush, lightly brush both sides of the slices and spread the garlic and herbs around on the bread. Wrap the bread in aluminum foil and bake at 350 degrees F for about 15 minutes. Serve warm.

Index